WILLIAM IVORY

William Ivory (aka Billy Ivory) is a British screenwriter, playwright and actor. He is a three-time BAFTA nominee and recipient of the Royal Television Society's Best Drama Series Award for *The Sins* in 2001.

He wrote the screenplays for the feature films *Made in Dagenham* (2010) and *The Great Escaper* (2023).

He was nominated for a television BAFTA for Best Drama Series for *Common As Muck* in 1995 and 1998 and for Best Drama Series for *The Sins* in 2001. *The Great Escaper* was nominated for Best British Film at the 2024 BAFTA film awards.

His other stage plays include *Diary of a Football Nobody* (2012), *Bomber's Moon* (2010) and *The Retirement of Tom Stevens* (2006).

William Ivory

THE MARKET DEEPING MODEL RAILWAY CLUB

NICK HERN BOOKS

London

www.nickhernbooks.co.uk

A Nick Hern Book

The Market Deeping Model Railway Club first published in Great Britain as a paperback original in 2026 by Nick Hern Books Limited, The Glasshouse, 49a Goldhawk Road, London

The Market Deeping Model Railway Club copyright © 2026 William Ivory

William Ivory has asserted his right to be identified as the author of this work

Cover image by AKA

Designed and typeset by Nick Hern Books, London
Printed in Great Britain by Mimeo Ltd, Huntingdon, Cambridgeshire PE29 6XX

A CIP catalogue record for this book is available from the British Library

ISBN 978 1 83904 597 4

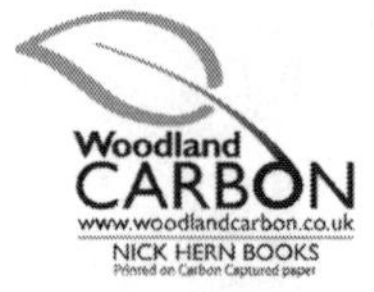

www.nickhernbooks.co.uk/environmental-policy

Nick Hern Books' authorised representative in the EU is
Easy Access System Europe – Mustamäe tee 50, 10621 Tallinn, Estonia
email gpsr.requests@easproject.com

The Market Deeping Model Railway Club was first performed at Nottingham Playhouse on 6 July 2026, with the following cast:

JORDAN	Babatunde Aléshé
CHRIS	Matt Bardock
GEORGE	Geoffrey Beevers
JERRY	Paul Bradley
NEIL	James Bradshaw
LINDA	Lucy Briers
GRAHAM	Adrian Scarborough
KEN	Deka Walmsley

Director	Adam Penford
Designer	Soutra Gilmour
Lighting Designer	Howard Hudson
Sound Designer and Composer	Alexandra Faye Braithwaite
Projection Designer	Jon Driscoll
Fight Director	Bret Yount
Voice and Dialect Coach	Kay Welch
Casting Director	Ginny Schiller CDG
Casting Assistant	Ben Armstrong
Associate Director	Hannah Stone
Associate Projection Designer	George Jarvis
Deputy Stage Manager	Rebecca Maltby
Assistant Stage Managers	Cormac O'Brien
	Leah Yates
Lighting Programmer	Tom Mulliner
Video Programmer	Dylan Marsh
Animator	Gemma Carrington

Supernumeraries   Jamie Adlam, Freya Allen, Joseph
Grainge, Margot Lubliner,
Guiseppe Manzione, Jessica
McWhirter, Christopher Molife,
Thomas Pears, Rory Squire,
Niamh Woolley

Characters

LINDA
JERRY
NEIL
GRAHAM
KEN
GEORGE
CHRIS
JORDAN

Notes

A slash (/) indicates an interruption.

An en dash (–) at the end of a line indicates an unfinished thought.

Whilst this play is inspired by real events, characters, names and events have been fictionalised for the purposes of the play.

This text went to press before the end of rehearsals and so may differ slightly from the play as performed.

ACT ONE

Scene One

May 22nd, 2018.

A room above a pub. Its walls are decorated with posters of railway companies, station signs and framed plans for point layouts.

Upstage centre, closed double doors lead to the stairs and have a wooden semaphore signal standing to one side of them. Its arm juts out horizontally, displaying a disc of red: STOP. An inner side door, also closed, is upstage right.

Upstage left is a sink, kettle and L-shaped work surface.

Downstage left is a high table with modelling materials on it.

Downstage right is a sofa, a luggage trunk – as casual table – and two tatty but rather comfy-looking armchairs. A bookshelf.

In the centre of the room, midway, is a round table (decorated to look like a goods yard wagon turntable) and six chairs.

LINDA, sixty, arranges notepads, paper and biros around the table.

She glances to the clock on the wall stage left (a large waiting room clock) and sees it is 7.28 p.m. She looks alarmed and scurries to pull a lever on the side of the semaphore mechanism. A bell pings, the arm drops, and a green disc is revealed: GO!

She ducks out, through the upstage-right side door.

The clock ticks to 7.30pm. Bang on cue, two men's voices are heard chanting, rather as a football crowd might –

NEIL *and* JERRY (*offstage*). We're Deepo, we've done it again! We're Deepo, we've done it again! We're –

The double doors fly open. A man of about forty, NEIL, enters. He wears a maroon sweatshirt with the MDMRC logo on its breast and his name woven beneath. He holds a rather modestly sized trophy, with a 'gold' locomotive sitting atop. The other side of the trophy is held by JERRY.

A third man, GRAHAM, sixties, grey-haired, wearing functional specs, and carrying a shoe box, enters.

GRAHAM. Lads, lads, lads, c'mon...! No triumphalism. It's not our way –

JERRY and NEIL are stunned. GRAHAM turns. He's joking. He's joking! He starts to chant too, and to conduct –

ALL. 'Cause we're Market Deeping. And we've done it again!

GRAHAM holds up a hand, then declaims –

GRAHAM. Winners of the Stamford Model Railway Exhibition 2018: Best Overall Layout in Show!

JERRY. Yes!

NEIL. Get in there!

NEIL carefully places the trophy on a table. And suddenly they stare as if at the Holy Grail –

GRAHAM. Oh, I know it's not all about winning but –

JERRY. Whoa! You must never say that. That's something I used to tell my people. In competition, it is *all* about winning. *Victori* Spolia.

JERRY nods, crosses to the kettle, picks it up, then moves to the tap –

GRAHAM. No. Right.

GRAHAM and NEIL lift out model pieces.

Does make next year's massive.

JERRY. What? Sorry – (*Indicates sink.*) Taps are still seized up.

NEIL *points to the award.*

NEIL. He means, if we get Best in Show again, we'll've done it three in a row. We get to keep the trophy.

JERRY (*to* GRAHAM, *excited*). You got something in mind?

Tries tap a final time. Gives up. Glances back.

GRAHAM. Just… ideas at the moment. No club's even come close before. But…

He slips a head torch in place, looks to JERRY.

That's for eight o'clock. Committee Meeting.

NEIL. Yeah but… Can't you tell us now?

GRAHAM (*smiles*). Ha! Wish I could only –

GRAHAM *holds up a small blue book.*

Club rules. Once something's on the agenda…

JERRY *nods; attends to his model now.*

JERRY. You gotta trust the process. I get that.

(*Glances to* GRAHAM.) It's something Jonny Wilkinson talks about a lot in his autobiography. Hell of a read.

CHRIS. Evenin'!

A man in his late fifties, CHRIS, *carrying two boxes, enters.*

He is wearing the requisite maroon sweatshirt. The lads mumble 'Chris' – but he's not listening, distracted by the trophy –

Oh, there she is… The pride of Lincolnshire! I could barely sleep last night. Thinkin' about us comin' away with that.

The others work – NEIL *slipping on a head torch, too –*

And they reckoned they had it in the bag, you know. NOB did.

GRAHAM. Chris, they're not called that.

CHRIS. What are they called?

GRAHAM. Northcott, Overton and Barrowby Model Railway
Club –

CHRIS. NOB.

(*To* NEIL.) Hey! I'm waiting for the day Casterton,
Uffington, Newbrough and Toft form a club. I'd have one of
their sweatshirts!

CHRIS *sniggers.* NEIL *too.*

Seriously though. They thought they'd stroll it – for that
layout of Ely Junction. The EM gauge.

NEIL. To be fair, the cathedral was lovely. And they'd got
terrific detail in the rolling stock –

CHRIS. Bollocks. They had the wrong roof colour on the
coaches and as for the cathedral! You see the Octagon? Was
way off. I measured it. Zero, zero two millimetres short at
the apex –

NEIL *makes to come back.*

The thing is, they're know-alls!!

Especially him, Murray, the chairman – you notice how he
talks? Like he's up in a pulpit –

GRAHAM. He's a vicar.

CHRIS (*slowed*). What, all the time?

GRAHAM *makes to affirm.*

He's a pain! End of!

CHRIS *looks round.*

Now, have we got the kettle on? Got a brew going?

NEIL. Can't. Taps're solid.

CHRIS. Oh. Fair dos. Anyway, I got me email – itinerary for
tonight – and I was *delighted* to see item four. Next Year's
Show… Or the hat trick-er as I like to think of it –

JERRY. Skip was just talking about that –

CHRIS. Well, there's big decisions to be made! Like… are we gonna get a cabinet built?

GRAHAM. What?

CHRIS. For the trophy. When it's ours to keep. Or will we take it in turns to have it at home? I'd love that up in my loft. Next to me layout there –

GRAHAM. I think we shouldn't jump the gun –

CHRIS. Gorra win first! I hear you! And step one's treadin' the opposition into the dirt!

He twinkles.

(*To* NEIL.) Provided you're happy with that, of course, Neil –

NEIL. What?

CHRIS *grins and pulls a* Daily Mail *from his bag-*

CHRIS. I meant to give you this last week – *Daily Mail* –

(*Turns to others.*) School in Birmingham; it's banned all competition – and not just sports: *everything*, even the chess club. So nobody ever loses and that way nobody's feelings ever get hurt!

CHRIS *scoffs.*

(*To* JERRY.) I mean, where's it gone? The country we grew up in. It's just bein'… PC'd into oblivion –

CHRIS *extends the paper.*

(*To* NEIL.) I thought you might fancy a read –

NEIL (*tightly*). I probably won't –

GRAHAM. Lads! Lads!

They turn. GRAHAM *has scooted to the round table and holds up the blue book again –*

Remember…? What we said… last time? Pullmans not politics. To prevent any further… misunderstandings?

CHRIS. Yeah. Course. Sorry… Sorry, Graham.

(*To* NEIL.) Sorry, mate. I just get frustrated sometimes-

CHRIS *opens the box. He pauses.*

That's when I have to say me mantra: 'This is why you model!' To remind yourself of a time when the world did make sense.

CHRIS *lifts out an O-gauge carriage from the 1940s.*

There you go. Von Ryan's Express.

GRAHAM. Oh, wow. Wow, Chris –

NEIL. That is good…

CHRIS *is proud but also a little embarrassed as the lads flock round his work.*

CHRIS. It's not bad, is it? Now it's varnished.

JERRY. What's it in?

CHRIS. One-sixty-fourth plywood. The bogies are Bachmann. The stanchions and springs I did on the lathe at work –

NEIL. What about your sprat and winkle? You cannibalised summat there or –

CHRIS. No! Be-spoke. Also. Directly off of the plans –

GRAHAM. There aren't any. It's a… war film –

CHRIS. Exactly. Shot in Italy. In which they used a Ferrovie della Stato Class 735 2-8-0 engine and this; which was a standard 1930s first-class coach, fitted with a fake end platform – required for the memorable and heart breakin' last scene in which Sinatra gets shot in the back by the chasin' Germans. And plans for them, for mid-century Italian passenger carriages, are indeed widely available on the net. If you dig a bit.

JERRY. Bloody hell…

NEIL. It's stunnin', mate. It's your best yet.

CHRIS (*taken aback*). Thank you. I… I mean –

CHRIS *picks up model, moves over to the rear prep area.*

I wanna put lamps on the tables. I… I feel it won't really cut the mustard till then. Mebbe napkins –

The centre doors crash open and GEORGE, *early eighties, staggers in, groaning.*

NEIL. Jesus!

GEORGE. Gents… Could someone…?

He's swaddled in a scarf, hat and a voluminous overcoat. He sways. The lads dash to him.

CHRIS. Flippin' heck, George! What's happened?

They half-carry him to the sofa.

GEORGE. Nothing. Just… Evensong ran over and…

Battery on the scooter died at the post office, so… I walked the rest of the way –

He starts to peel off the layers of clothing.

CHRIS. You shoulda rung! We'd've come and got you –

GEORGE. I… I fancied a stroll to be honest. So mild…

NEIL. Yeah… You don't think you're overdressed, do you? Early summer?

GEORGE. It's for the way back. When it gets cooler. Doc said I needed to be careful. Since the pneumonia.

NEIL. Right.

GEORGE. I'm okay… It was the stairs… Got half way up and then… The angina kicked in…

GEORGE *pulls out a small spray and squirts under his tongue.*

CHRIS. You sure you should'a come at all, George?

GEORGE. Course I should! I told you. I'm fine.

GEORGE *stands. Collapses again.*

Oh… Vertigo!

He pops a different pill. Stands once more. Takes a step.

There! Never better! Now, what are we doing…? Ooh. Carflat Wagon –

He picks up a small car transporter at JERRY*'s spot.*

JERRY. Graham Farish. Got it on eBay. You don't often see 'em in N-gauge. It's missing the bogie coupling but I can replace that.

GEORGE. Nineteen sixty-eight?

JERRY. Seven.

GEORGE. Knew it! I worked with the real ones! They were all across Southern –

He chuckles; distracted.

Oh! Chris! The Von Ryan!

CHRIS. What do you think? Alright?

GEORGE. It's magnificent!

(*Leans closer.*) Have you thought about netting for the luggage racks?

CHRIS. Exactly!! See? See! He's got it! And that's why the Market Deeping Model Railway Club keeps coming away with that thing!

He points to trophy.

'Cause we all know:

ALL. The Devil's in the Detail!

They all laugh and grin!

KEN. What's funny?

KEN, *about sixty, fit, stands by the open side door. He looks a tad stern. All laughter stops.*

GRAHAM. Ken. I didn't realise you were here.

KEN. Yeah. I came up the back stairs. I wanted five minutes next door, on the test track… See if I could suss out what the problem was. From the weekend.

GEORGE. This is… Woodcroft, is it, Ken? I can't believe you had to withdraw it again. It must be the unluckiest layout in the world!

KEN. Thanks, George. I… I think it was the points now. Just outside me fiddle yard. Everything else seems fine.

GEORGE. Aaah. Well, they're notorious, Ken, points! Key thing's not to let it frustrate you. Now you're so close to… *finally* unveiling her – in all her glory!!

KEN *stares, nods. Then, he looks to* GRAHAM.

KEN. I need to get a jig, from the car. I won't be long.

He leaves. The men get to their modelling tasks.

GEORGE. I feel so sorry for him! Woodcroft! ANOTHER withdrawal, and when he was… CERTAIN this time, that she was ready to show… Oh well! He'll get there.

CHRIS. Yeah. Right.

His scorn is obvious. NEIL *notes it, then looks to the door.*

NEIL. He is a powerful man, inni? Ken.

GRAHAM. What?

NEIL. I'm sayin', for his age. He's still powerful… And he's got an aura about him. He does scare me a bit, to be honest.

JERRY. Well, he killed a man.

GRAHAM. We don't know that!

JERRY. Yes, we do! He was a soldier! He got a medal. It won't've been for crocheting, will it? You get medals in the army for killing people –

GEORGE. Je-rry! Graham's right. We mustn't… jump to conclusions. He could've got it for any number of reasons.

JERRY *stares pointedly.*

Like… marching or… doing a good salute! Anything like
that –

GRAHAM. At the same time, I am relieved he didn't come in
a second later. I was about to ask you, Chris: did you look
into that sound card. For George's Victoria Station layout?

CHRIS. Yeah! And he needs two. First one's for the rolling
stock and the second'll do all the ambient noise: station
announcements, newspaper sellers, that sort of thing. But
they're both Bluetooth controlled, from the same app, on the
same tablet.

GEORGE. Oh, Graham. It's astonishing. When you think how
far we've come –

He points to the others.

And I'm bound to say: I think you're misjudging Ken –
about the new technology –

CHRIS. Misjudging!? Don't you remember? When digital first
came out, and Neil got that DCC trial version? Ken chucked
his iPad out the window –

JERRY (*muttering, to* NEIL). Very 'number one saluter', that –

CHRIS (*nodding*). Unless you use analogue, Ken goes ape –

JERRY. In which case, he's his own worst enemy. Adapt or die.
That's the maxim we had to live by in business. And it's no
less true for us here… That's why we've got Earl Grey as
well as builder's. You have to move with the times.

NEIL. You don't, though, do you? In model railwaying. That's
the whole point. You find a time you like and you stick
with it.

JERRY (*to* NEIL). Well, if we want to *stay* top of the pile,
we're gonna *have to* evolve!

GEORGE (*not really listening*). Hear, hear! Is anybody getting
the kettle on?

CHRIS. Can't. Taps're stuck.

GEORGE. Ah. Right… And what about the kitchen? How's the mould looking?

JERRY. We haven't flipped a coin yet.

GEORGE. Well… why don't we get a pint, instead?

GRAHAM. What?

GEORGE. Adjourn downstairs.

CHRIS. That's not a bad idea.

GRAHAM. But… It's modelling time…

The lads are moving.

What are you doing? We've barely started –

NEIL. Drink's a drink, innit?

CHRIS. And we could have the committee meeting down there, too, if we wanted –

GRAHAM. That's not till eight!

NEIL. Yeah. Change of scenery.

Might encourage some of that… what's-it, you're always banging on about –

JERRY. Blue sky thinking. Absolutely.

GRAHAM. Men –

He stands and takes a step towards the door – and the ongoing exodus.

Hang on…

GEORGE. Just need an itinerary!

He grabs one from the table, pleased, and goes.

GRAHAM. Wait –

They've already disappeared down the stairs.

We've tried the bar! It didn't work. We didn't finish till two in the morning… Men –

No response.

Men!!

He waves his rule book, miffed.

You're freestyling!

'We Are the Champions' by Queen rings out, once, from the bar doors below. GRAHAM hesitates, and finally, runs after the others. At the same time, a voice calls out:

LINDA (*offstage*). Graham! Graham, I'm back –

Bursts through side door.

Got boxed in by the bloody Brownies–

She halts, looks around, confused and calls out:

Graham…? Anyone?

She notices the meeting table and everything she had prepared – now in disarray. She exhales. She crosses and grabs the kettle. She turns on the tap. Water gushes out, into the kettle.

Blackout.

Scene Two

GRAHAM *glides into view through a trap door in the floor.*

He is surrounded by shelves, books, railway ephemera and his home layout – which he stands at the centre of. He watches a train running along the track. There is a tap from below.

GRAHAM. Hello…?

LINDA (*offstage*). Are you there?

GRAHAM. Yes. Course. Come up…

He waits. But nothing happens.

Linda?

LINDA (*offstage*). You're standing on the trap.

He realises and moves away. The lid lifts and she climbs up. She is wearing a dressing gown and fluffy slippers. He is about to speak when the train stops.

GRAHAM. Oooh. Points… hang on –

He flips a switch on a control console. The train carries on.

There… It's funny you know, we were talking about analogue earlier. The old ways, like this… loads of cabling under your baseboard and… stacks of push-to-make buttons; I do understand why Ken likes the traditional ways. It's as if, over the years, you add… layers of skin to a basic skeleton. Whereas, digital, it's so easy just to try out a *new* configuration. You download a virtual layout builder, and it'll tell you: whether your track, your rolling stock, your points are gonna work together before you've even got started!

He looks at her with something close to incredulity.

LINDA. It's four in the morning, Graham.

GRAHAM. What?

LINDA. Four… a.m.… I woke up for the loo and… I went past your room, and I could see: the bed hadn't been slept in.

GRAHAM. Right. It's the adrenaline. After a club night. Especially if we've got the monthly committee meeting as well. I think most people would struggle in those circumstances. Sports performers are exactly the same. Jonny Wilkinson didn't sleep for three days after England won the Rugby World Cup. Apparently.

LINDA. Yes, well, eighty thousand spectators, an extra time, match-winning kick, I can see how that might leave you a bit overstimulated.

GRAHAM. Is this because we decamped to the bar? Without informing you – as club secretary.

LINDA. No –

GRAHAM. Look, Linda, we appreciate what you do for us. But it's *you* that insists on having all of the responsibility and none of the joy. We want you to be involved the way we are…! Crikey, Chris bought you that… bespoke container, to put scalpel blades in and… I have to be honest, I remember your response was a little ungracious –

LINDA. Ungracious? He covered a tobacco tin with floral sticky-backed plastic and gave it to me with a card which said: 'Bogies aren't just for Boys'! Germaine Greer was my tutor at university, Graham!!

He blinks. She stops, and counts to three. Then:

I'm really not interested in modelling, thank you… I *am* interested in going back to bed. There's pork pie in the fridge if you decide to push through.

He's slightly lost.

We've got an early start in the morning. I'd prefer it if you were fuelled.

Now he's entirely lost. And she sees it.

GRAHAM. What are – ?

LINDA. Maria's funeral.

GRAHAM. Oh, God. Yes. I'd forgotten… And we should definitely go, shouldn't we?

LINDA. Graham!

GRAHAM. I'm just… It *is* a long way and it must be eight or nine years since we last saw her –

LINDA. She was our neighbour for a quarter of a century. And I'm sure Malcolm would appreciate our presence.

GRAHAM. Malcolm? I thought he was already dead?

LINDA. No. That's Roger. On the other side… Moved to Devon.

GRAHAM. Bloody hell… you get to our age and… it's carnage… It makes you think.

He does. Then turns and grabs another engine from a shelf. He considers where to place it. She watches him.

LINDA. It makes me think, I miss weddings. Everyone's nicely boozy, aren't they, and full of largesse. There's always a good chance of intrigue or… people getting caught in flagrante. But by and large, weddings are the domain of young people. And the only light buffets we get to enjoy these days are at wakes – where generally, people feel less inclined to have it off.

GRAHAM. Linda!

LINDA. I'm sorry. I… I –

She's checked herself. But his look is of SUCH incomprehension, that she thrums again.

I'm upset…! *That* is why I'm… a little voluble, shall we say.

GRAHAM. About what?

LINDA. About… the way you treat me.

GRAHAM. What? Generally?

LINDA. No. I –

She thinks; pushes on.

I mean, in committee meetings. You make me feel… completely peripheral.

GRAHAM. How do I? I –

LINDA. AOB! Any other business!!

She pulls a clutch of letters from her dressing-gown pocket.

You swore you would mention these this time. You promised me!

GRAHAM. And… I would have…! Except for George! And the pork scratching. You saw the colour he went! When his health is NOT good! To be honest, I thought we were in Heimlich territory –

LINDA. The club's going to be evicted, Graham! You've been served notice. And you *need* to share that news with the membership. *Or* let the club secretary share it, given she's the one the brewery keeps writing to –

GRAHAM. How could I?! I mean, really, Linda, if we're laying our cards on the table, how? On the night when we were discussing the opportunity we now have to win Best in Show for a third year running and to carve our names into Eastern Counties model railwaying folklore? Can you imagine what that does to a man?! Which is why there *was* a *particularly* febrile atmosphere this evening, and why any further stimulation… well… the mind boggles, frankly… What? Why are you looking at me like that?

LINDA (*smiling*). Because I always forget… how animated you become. About club matters.

GRAHAM. Well, I apologise but… I feel extremely strongly about it.

LINDA. I know. But you need to tell them the truth, Graham. Please.

Blackout.

Scene Three

'Up Yer Bum' by Peter and the Test Tube Babies. Very loud.

Lights up.

January 10th, 2019.

It is dark in the club room. But a glow bleeds through from the kitchen area. KEN appears wearing woolly hat, fingerless mittens, and a face mask. He crosses to the modelling table, takes out a pair of pliers and exits. LINDA enters with a carrier bag. She switches on the lights. Christmas decorations still hang from some of the fittings. The round table has been replaced by a large oblong shape resting on trestle legs and covered by a sheet. LINDA *shifts the signal to green.*

LINDA. Ken. Ken! Keeeeen!!

The music stops. He appears through the side door.

KEN. I'm sorry. I didn't hear –

He stops, removes face mask.

I didn't realise the time.

LINDA. It gets dark so early, you lose track, don't you…? How was your Christmas?

KEN. It was quiet. Just me but… I don't mind that. How was yours?

LINDA. Lovely. Thank you. Jonathan visited. With the grandchildren.

KEN. Did they stop long?

LINDA. Just Boxing Day. Then back to Reading… Why are you – ?

She indicates the mask he now holds.

KEN. Oh, it's the stuff Chris's mate's put on the walls –

LINDA. The anti-fungal? Is it…?

KEN. Hard to say. You still can't really breath near it. But… it was free wannit, so…

LINDA. I suppose any improvement's a step in the right direction.

She points beyond the door.

Who was that? The music.

KEN. Peter and the Test Tube Babies.

LINDA. Ah. What was it called?

KEN. 'Up Yer Bum'.

LINDA. No, I don't know that.

They both laugh.

Right. I better get the oven on –

She taps the carrier bag.

Pizza. Graham said it could be a long one –

She points to the trestle.

You need to break the back of Frodingham – I did say to him: Why start a *completely* new club effort when you've surely got old layouts you could adapt and take some of the pressure off?

KEN *smiles, extends a hand.*

KEN. No. No. Not when there's so much at stake. I dunno if he's mentioned it but if the club –

LINDA. Wins Best in Show a third time… Yes, it has cropped up.

KEN (*laughing*). Right. Well, Graham took the view, whatever we're doin' with our own, individual, layouts, the Club display – that's goin' for the big prize – *that* has got to be something special.

LINDA. Is it?

KEN. It's not lookin' bad. It's about the fine detail… Like Jerry says: genius is the infinite capacity for pain… Summat like that.

LINDA. He's got rather a lot of those up his sleeve hasn't he, Jerry? Ooh. I need to give you one of these –

She pulls a sheet of paper from her satchel.

It's week by week, right up to the show. Everyone's tasks and responsibilities re. the club display –

She points to sheeted display.

And the bit at the bottom's a tear-off. To go back to Graham so he can vector in *precisely* where people are with their own layouts –

She blinks, shifts. Then she tries to be matter of fact.

You know… having them show ready.

(*Quieter.*) In case anyone needs help.

KEN. Yeah. I'll… Ta.

He folds it and slips it in his pocket. He starts to move.

LINDA. How is yours, Ken? How's… Woodcroft looking?

KEN. It's almost there… I'm not sayin' it's completely done but… I'll start… bringin' it in soon – in sections. To work on here.

LINDA. That's wonderful.

KEN. I was *so* close last year, Linda! To gerrin' it out there – exhibitin' it. Only, since then it's felt like one setback after another. Your transformer breaks down, your tender comes off its bogie –

LINDA. Your sound card stops working.

KEN. What?

LINDA. I don't know why I said that. I –

She starts to move off. He reaches out – she smiles, rictus.

KEN. Oh, come on, Linda, not you 'n'all?! I have *not* got a problem with digital.

That iPad goin' out the window was a one off! 'Cause… no one was being honest. I like traditional. They wanna go more modern. Fine. Agree to disagree.

LINDA. They know that now –

KEN. They think I'm a psycho.

LINDA. They do not! I've never heard *any* of them talk about you in that way –

KEN. I bet they've said stuff about Woodcroft – that I'm *never* gonna show it. 'Cause there's *always* gonna be problems! I bet they've said that.

She laughs. It's not convincing.

LINDA. Never.

He stares; knows she's watching their backs. Then he nods and steps closer –

KEN. You believe me, though, Linda, don't you? That I *am* gonna get there. In the end.

LINDA. I know you are, Ken. I *know* you'll show it.

He stares. She really does believe it. And he smiles, suddenly lighter. She smiles, too.

Right. Oven!

KEN. Here. You'll need this.

He passes her a mask. She turns.

What sort of music do you like? I used to listen to them –

He jabs a thumb to the kitchen.

– all the time in the army. Thing is, I don't think you ever grow out what you were first into when you were young, do you?

LINDA. No. I think you're right.

KEN *shrugs: so?*

Oh. David Bowie… T-Rex, Roxy Music… This was when I was first at uni. I think I really just liked any group with a handsome singer who wore make-up! Actually, I quite liked Bob Dylan, too, and I think he was largely eyeliner free. But then I had Jonathan…

And it was more, incy-wincy spider round the clock… I do enjoy house music, though.

KEN. What?!

LINDA. I know! It's because I had a girlfriend I… went on walking trips with, back in the nineties, and she played it all the time.

KEN. Ha! Linda Collinson… Our secret raver –

LINDA. Stop it! Though to be honest, Ken… time does seem to just… accelerate beyond a certain point. I remember my mother saying that and thinking: 'Oh Mum, stop going on!' And then one day you wake up and… you're old!

She laughs but looks momentarily exposed. Then NEIL *and* JERRY *enter. Cries of 'Alright' and 'Happy New Year'. But both are in business mode and move straight to the modelling bench where they dump their boxes.* LINDA *beams at them.*

Gents! Schedules. Up to the show –

She places the sheets down and heads for the side door, donning the mask.

JERRY. Right! Straight to it! Come on. Let's get the sheet off –

The others join him.

One, two, three!

They lift it away. An impressive new layout lies beneath – plenty looking finished. In beautiful gold lettering, on dark varnished wood, is written: 'FRODINGHAM, MPD 1953 – MARKET DEEPING MODEL RAILWAY CLUB'. Much nodding and cooing ensues –

KEN. Hey. He's got the sign done!

NEIL. Frodingham MPD, 1953 – Market Deeping Model Railway Club… That is nice!

JERRY. Absolutely. Much to be pleased with… But remember: success is a ladder you cannot climb with your hands in your pockets.

KEN. What?

JERRY. It's a proverb. Always said it to my people when we'd had a good quarter… So they'd not rest on their laurels.

The doors bash open. GRAHAM *props up a swooning* GEORGE.

GRAHAM. Lads. Can you… just – ?!

KEN. Whoa! George –?

NEIL. What's happened now?!

They sit GEORGE *down –*

GEORGE. It's alright. I'm alright. Really. I… took a wrong pill…

Cries of 'What'? from the group.

For the cat. Wormer. But it set my heart off like a Buddy Rich drum solo…

GEORGE *groans, stands. Then takes off his coat.*

It's gone. It's gone. I'm fine… I'm like Lazarus.

He chuckles and removes another two coats.

KEN. How many of those have you got on?

GEORGE. Sufficient…

GEORGE *is distracted by the layout.*

Oh. Oh, the sign!! Frodingham Motive Power Depot!

He looks round and beams.

By the A Team!

CHRIS *slides in, carrying a large box.*

CHRIS. Alright, lads? Happy New Year.

GEORGE. Chris! Have you seen this?

CHRIS. Yeah. It's nice.

He sounds tight. Like HIS Christmas wasn't great. He gets his Von Ryan out of his box.

GEORGE. It's a bit better than that!

GRAHAM. It's bang on schedule. I think that's the important thing. Apropos of which, I dunno if Linda's mentioned but can you all, please, grab one of these… there's a bit at the bottom I'd like you to take particular notice of in case you're having any issues –

Suddenly staring at KEN.

– with your own layouts. In which case –

Looking anywhere but KEN.

Fill 'em in, anyway.

KEN. I'm paintin' some baseboards in the car park. Shout me if you need me.

He walks out. GRAHAM *stares helplessly at the door.*

NEIL. Just ask him! 'Where are you with Woodcroft?'

GRAHAM. I can't! It implies doubt –

NEIL. There is doubt! And it's your job! You're chairman.

CHRIS. I'll speak to him. We still haven't told him 'bout the effects we're addin' to that, have we?

He points to Frodingham.

The tool shed sounds… the foundry smoke and… that is my department so…

He delves in box and removes a small plastic item.

I did manage to get a cartridge for the smoke, by the way. You can't normally buy this kind over here – load a health and safety bollocks only I've got a mate works in China so he's sorted us out.

NEIL. But… what's in it? Health and safety, they –

CHRIS. They're a joke, that's what they are! Top of the tree in the bleedin' Nanny State!

He hammers a section of track. Rather harder than he needs to. Everyone stares. And GRAHAM *pushes on.*

GRAHAM. Right. And… were you able to… source the sound cards, Chris? Was that successful?

CHRIS *looks up. He calms.*

CHRIS. Yeah. Plus, I got the two George needs. For his Victoria Station –

GEORGE. Oh, thank you! Thank you, Chris. And what did you decide to do about Von Ryan in the end?

CHRIS (*nods*). I think it'll work.

GRAHAM. What will? Sorry, I –

GEORGE. You were there, Graham! When we discussed it…

If he was, GRAHAM *cannot remember it –*

If Chris models the chasing pack of German soldiers and has a Sinatra figurine, too, then he can actually remount the last scene of the film! And show Frank being gunned down by the Gestapo, even as salvation, in the form of the train, lies in sight. And the chip thing will allow him to add in the sound of the machine guns *and* the Nazi jackboots. He can even have Frank's death-rattle!

He beams. GRAHAM *stares for half a second and nods –*

GRAHAM. I see. I didn't realise you were being serious –

GEORGE. And vis-á-vis Frank –

He rummages in his pocket and produces a figurine.

The scale's spot-on! I checked!

GRAHAM. What is it?

GEORGE. Bride and groom! It was on our wedding cake. Mine and Gwen's. But then she decided to bake a Victoria sponge for Harry and Meghan's big day, so I hacksawed 'em apart –

He pulls the figures asunder.

– so I could ginger up his hair a bit and that means *now* he can easily be repainted – so his Blues and Royals go nicely Nazi!

There is a murmur of approval. NEIL *takes the figurine.*

GRAHAM. Lads…

NEIL. His face isn't unlike Sinatra's, is it? Harry's.

GRAHAM. Lads…

JERRY *takes the figurine.*

JERRY. I reckon you could pull it off –

GRAHAM. Lads!!

They all lean in.

Sorry. You are sure… you wanna… definitely go for that level of detail?

JERRY. Why not?

GRAHAM. Well, modern times. Modern sensibilities. I mean, is that something, which, today, you… we… as a club, want to capture? And… immortalise?

NEIL. It's one of the great scenes in the canon of World War Two action movies –

GRAHAM. I know! I know. I just… wonder what… a German might think? Say. Whether they might find it… a bit offensive?

CHRIS. Are you serious?

JERRY. It's just a layout, skip.

NEIL. Actually, I do see what he's getting at now –

CHRIS. Of course you do.

NEIL. What's that mean?

CHRIS. Graham, if the Germans were that worried about future generations gerrin' upset by an exhibit at the Stamford Model Railway Annual Show, they should never've set about establishin' the Third Reich, should they?!

GRAHAM. Please! You're –

CHRIS. I mean, when, precisely, *did* you decide, The Market Deeping Model Railway Club had to go woke.

JERRY. What – ?

GEORGE. Chris –

CHRIS. He's gone and thrown his hat in the ring with his lot!

(*Pointing to* NEIL.) – The reds. And when I say reds, I don't mean Nottingham Forest –

NEIL. My lot? Wh–?

He steps closer to CHRIS. GRAHAM *scrambles for the rule book.*

GRAHAM. Boys! Boys! Please!! We were of… one accord! We will *not* be going down that particular rabbit hole ever again! Not when we are a… strictly non-affiliated, non-aligned, non-sectarian, model railwaying club –

He taps the page in his book.

It's all in the rules!

CHRIS *stares – for a long moment.*

CHRIS. Fine… Fine… I just hate the way our… history is gradually bein' turned into something we have to be… ashamed of –

NEIL *makes to speak.*

But! I'm not gonna make a big thing of it. There's no need now, anyway. Not since we've took back control –

NEIL. Awww –

GRAHAM. No! No!

NEIL. You can't help yourself –

GRAHAM. Not the B-word.

He holds up rule book again.

Not allowed –

CHRIS. It matters! This proves it does!

GEORGE. Actually, men –

CHRIS. And fifty-two per cent of the country agrees with me –

NEIL. As opposed to the forty-eight per cent –

JERRY. Guys! On this one –

CHRIS. Win's a win, mate! And anyway, it was nearer sixty per cent round here – seventy-five when you get up to Boston. In fact, I think they came in at number one –

NEIL. Number one?! It isn't *Top of the Pops*, you twat!

CHRIS. Oh, here we go!

GEORGE (*to* GRAHAM). Do you think we should perhaps adjourn downstairs?

NEIL. And what about the three hundred and fifty million quid for the NHS? Have you asked the people of Boston how they feel about that; now it's all just… disappeared –

CHRIS. They didn't mean *actual* money –

NEIL. Well, what the fuck did they mean, then?!

GEORGE *turns to the double doors.*

GRAHAM. George. Hang on!… Boys. Look. Look, what you're doing!

CHRIS. It's him… he just can't accept that the man in the street's had enough of bein' dictated to by a bunch of foreigners –

NEIL. What are you talkin' about?

CHRIS. Bein' told what hours we can or can't work! Or what rules apply in a British court. Or –

(*Points to carriage.*) Whether it's acceptable to see Frank Sinatra gunned down by a bunch of the Waffen fucking SS!!

NEIL *scoffs, stunned.*

Just tell me: are you happy to eat straight bananas?

NEIL. There are no straight bananas –

CHRIS. No?

NEIL. No!!

CHRIS. Well, if there was, I tell you where the first one'd be going –

GRAHAM *slams his hand on table.*

GRAHAM. Stop it!! Both of you!! This is completely unacceptable!!

CHRIS *and* NEIL *look over, stunned.*

I'm sorry to raise my voice. I hate doing it. I was the same in the classroom. But sometimes… with the rowdy boys –

GRAHAM *stops, takes a deep breath.*

The point being… I am the chairman of this organisation and as such, I do hold some sway, so… I'm suspending club night! Until we've had a… a little intermission… downstairs. Perhaps, Chris, you could lead the way –

CHRIS *prickles.*

Going alphabetically…! In thirty-second intervals.

CHRIS *thunders out.* NEIL *instantly steps closer.*

NEIL. That was him, Graham. I swear! I mean, how do you make the annual show about Brexit? He's –

GRAHAM. He's under a lot of stress!! And we need to cut him some slack.

Everyone hears the note and glances are exchanged.

JERRY. Why? What's happened?

GRAHAM. It's Andrew. He bailed again.

NEIL. What?

GRAHAM. Christmas Day. He texted apparently. Something had came up.

NEIL. On Christmas Day?

GRAHAM. I know. I know.

Much scoffing and tutting. GEORGE *glances to* JERRY.

GEORGE. I tell you, if that boy was my son –

GRAHAM. To be fair, George, Andrew is still feeling the effects of the divorce.

JERRY. Well, he needs to man up! He's twenty-five!

NEIL. On top of which, it wasn't his dad's fault! It was his mum who ran off – with that bloke with a personalised number plate –

GEORGE. And a Nespresso machine.

NEIL. So if anyone should still be feeling it, it's Chris! It's him that needs supportin'!

(*Hears himself.*) Oh, bloody hell… I'll go and buy him a bag of salt and vinegar…

NEIL *moves, stops then turns.*

Thing is, he can be a complete nob at times but… it's the principle, innit? All for one and for all! It's the main reason I joined the club. To feel like I was… back in a gang at school. Though to be honest, I never really had that where I went. I used to get beat up every break. Boys and girls.

He remembers – then continues to the door.

GEORGE. Wait! I'll come with you… I think my pacemaker is trying to pair with one of these new soundcards… I need to be careful around Bluetooth –

He nods towards the worktop, jovialy.

I mean, here we are imagining Frank dropping to the floor and turning up his toes when, in fact –

He places his hands above chest.

Dzzzzzzr!

GRAHAM. Go! Now!!! Quickly –

He herds them to stairs.

I'll make sure they're well out of the way before you come back!

They leave. GRAHAM *looks across to* JERRY. *He sighs –*

Christ… One minute you're… And then the next you're…

And the thing is, we can't have this sort of rancour – not if we want to be… modern and… welcoming… Encourage fresh membership.

JERRY. That's… something we're trying to do, is it?

GRAHAM. Yes! We haven't had anybody new come on board for eleven years now, Jerry…! I've been thinking about it.

A lot. Because extra subs could be very useful in the future if –

He slows, realising the territory he's entered.

You know… we have to… adapt to any… changes in our circumstances. Say.

JERRY. What changes? I –

GRAHAM. Legacy! It's more… that. Where is the *next* generation of model railwayers, Jerry. Those who might… *broaden* our current membership demographic.

JERRY. When you say our *current* membership demographic…?

GRAHAM. Old, white and male.

JERRY. No, it's not.

GRAHAM. It is quite.

JERRY. Neil's forty-five.

GRAHAM. To someone in their twenties –

JERRY. What about Linda?

GRAHAM. She's sixty!

JERRY. She's not a man.

GRAHAM. She's not a member!

He clarifies.

She's admin! She doesn't model.

JERRY. Okay, well… In that case, I'm gonna address the elephant in the room… What if we are… what you say? Old and white and men. That's not a bad thing, is it? Even if I'll likely be dead in the next eight to eleven-and-a-quarter years according to the Office for National Statistics, I… I still have value. I mean, I *do* have value, Graham.

He looks right at GRAHAM. It feels less like a statement and more of a plea for affirmation. GRAHAM straightens.

GRAHAM. Of course you do, Jerry. That's… a given. I'm simply keen we should share all of this – not the mould – with new talent. That's all it is!

JERRY isn't convinced. GRAHAM shoves a twenty pound note out.

Here! Why don't you go and get us both a single malt. Aged AND revered! I'll be down in a second –

JERRY stares, nods, and finally leaves. GRAHAM sighs.

God help me.

He runs across, shoves the sound chips in a metal box, then hurries to the stairs. He stops – shouts to the side door:

Linda… Pizza delivery time! Put it back half an hour. There's been an insurrection!

He moves the signal to red, and goes. A beat.

LINDA enters carrying a tower of cooked pizzas. She wears an old Walkman CD player and headset. She frowns and looks round. Odd. She places the pizzas down and again scans the room. There is a glint in her eye and she turns up the Walkman. We hear what she's listening to, getting louder: 'Show Me Love' by Robin S. Then she starts to dance. She moves beautifully – rhythmic and fluid and young. The music grows louder. She raises her arms wide, and turns her face to heaven, as if in ecstasy –

Blackout.

Scene Four

Lights up.

May 1st, 2019.

GEORGE *embellishes a section of Victoria Station.* CHRIS *and* NEIL *are hard at Frodingham.* GRAHAM *ticks his clipboard.*

KEN *enters from the side room and asks what he can do to help.* GRAHAM *indicates Frodingham needs more manpower. Music fades and* CHRIS *stops work, smiling –*

CHRIS. This is gonna be our best year yet.

He inhales.

I can smell it.

GEORGE. That's the anti-fungal, Chris. It really is quite pungent, still… Did your friend say we should leave the window open?

KEN. No. No! George. That's the chilli. What you're getting a whiff of. Linda's warming the scran through –

NEIL. Is our stand for Frodingham, the same place as last year? 'Cause the light in there's brilliant –

GRAHAM (*taps clipboard*). Hall One, stand eleven.

GRAHAM *beams. His phone rings – with a steam train whistle.*

Hang on. That's mine –

KEN *sees it and picks it up, checking the screen.*

KEN. It's Frank. In the bar.

GRAHAM. Ah. Right…

GRAHAM *takes the phone.*

Frank…? I see. Okay. I'll nip down –

(*To the lads.*) Won't be long.

He goes. CHRIS *glances up from his endeavours.*

CHRIS. I'll be skippin' the food tonight, lads. Need to leave room for later –

No one responds: all hard at it again. CHRIS *looks peeved. Like he might say more but then the doors fly open.*

JERRY. Gentle-Men! Good evening… Good evening, one and all! How are we? How's it all going?

JERRY puts his box down, points to the main display.

Frodingham MPD, 1953. And it bloody well is! That is genius.

He opens his box flamboyantly.

NEIL. Are you alright, Jerry?

JERRY. Never better, Neil. Thank you…

JERRY swallows.

Actually, I wouldn't mind –

He grabs a mug, looks to the tap, replaces the mug.

I'm gonna concentrate on my own layout, tonight. If that's okay? Got an app, obvs, task manager –

He pulls out his phone.

– and it's told me I'm eleven hours behind. Course, you model in N, it's fiddly. Does take longer. But that's the challenge.

KEN. You sure you're okay, mate?

JERRY seems wrong-footed by the question.

CHRIS. Jerry… I was just tellin' the lads: I won't be eatin' with you tonight. 'Cause Andrew's comin' up!

The lads do re-engage. CHRIS hides his pleasure.

I've… booked us into Hambleton Hall. Sod it. He'll be used to nice stuff from London and… Everywhere else round here, it's alright but it's like he says, it's 'cause we don't know any better.

GEORGE. Oh, well. That's terrific, Chris. Do send him our regards –

CHRIS. I will! I will do!

GRAHAM steps back into the room. JERRY salutes.

JERRY. Skipper!

GRAHAM is distracted.

GRAHAM. Jerry. I –

He re-focuses.

Could I have everyone's attention, please? I'm delighted to say that earlier this week I received an email from somebody enquiring about the possibility of joining the club – as its newest member! So, naturally enough, I invited them along!

He turns, hand out. No one's there. He looks round the door.

Sorry. I thought you'd just come through –

JORDAN, *a fresh-faced young man enters. He is a person from the global majority.*

This is Jordan, everyone. Jordan this is the… Market Deeping Model Railway Club!

The lads absorb him. He's MUCH younger and much less white.

JORDAN. Alright.

They all mumble salutations…

GRAHAM. Jordan's from London. He recently graduated from university there. His family has just moved up this way and… well, obviously, he needs to feel that we're a good fit for him, so tonight, before he makes any… *final* decisions, Jordan's gonna have a… no-strings-attached, 'this is who we are' look around the facilities.

GRAHAM smiles; waits for a more articulated greeting.

JERRY. Good! Bloody good. Hmmm? Welcome Jordan. Welcome to the MDMRC!

JERRY puts an arm round JORDAN's shoulders.

Let me show you this: This is Frodingham Motive Power Depot, 1953. Modelled in double-oh scale. Which is actually a scale generally only used in this country because –

JORDAN. Track-size difference. Yeah. I know. The sixteen-point-five millimetre gauge which double-oh employs is actually the correct measurement for the slightly smaller HO scale, popular in continental Europe and the USA.

But British model manufacturers in the 1930s found that all the electric motors available at the time were too large to fit the true-to-scale British locos, so they simply enlarged the model bodies – to 1:76 scale – whilst keeping the gauge of the track at the HO standard. Which was 1:87.

CHRIS. Bloody hell, you're perfect.

CHRIS *moves over and pumps* JORDAN*'s hand. The others join.*

GRAHAM. Okay, boys, don't crowd him. Let him breathe.

JORDAN. It's fine! It's nice to be made welcome…

GEORGE. Well, you are! We've never had anyone like you before.

Everyone looks to GEORGE.

So young! It's a breath of fresh air!

KEN. You been modelling long?

JORDAN. Not really. They had a Rail Soc at university and I'm not that bothered about sport, so, I just… thought I'd give it a go.

GRAHAM. Well, we'd be delighted to continue your education, so to speak –

(*Adamant.*) – though, no pressure. The choice is entirely yours –

GEORGE. We are very good though –

JORDAN. I know! I saw this copy of the *Railway Modeller* just before we moved. They went round all the regional shows… and they talked about you. You're on for the hat trick, aren't you?

GRAHAM. Yes! Yes, we are.

CHRIS. Oh, mate…! I wish I was stayin' tonight, I really do. Only, Graham, I was sayin', I'm seein' Andrew. We're goin' out.

JERRY. The thing is, Jordan, the key thing, now, in making your decision, is to understand that your jam, is our jam! You feel me?

JORDAN. What?

JERRY. Because I'm certain, at one level, you're looking at us and thinking: 'Hmm. I'm not so sure. Bunch of old blokes.' But! Know this: we are not out of touch. We're *in* touch. In fact, *most* of us here still pay for our prescriptions.

He beams, eyes slightly crazed.

GRAHAM. Everything alright, Jerry?

NEIL. He's fine. Apparently.

JERRY *abruptly returns to his bench, and starts to work.*

GRAHAM. Okay…! Jordan! This is the main club room… Out there we have a small kitchen and a test track – where members can try out their rolling stock. Currently it also houses many of the… individual displays we'll be exhibiting *at* the annual… Eastern get-together – Frodingham being the club offering and the layout which we hope *will* be enough to win us that historic, third, Best in Show.

CHRIS. We'll be going neck and neck with our main rivals, NOB.

GRAHAM. Chr-is!

JORDAN. Why are they called NOB?

GRAHAM (*glares at* CHRIS). It's… an acronym –

JERRY. Like a cock. He means nob like a cock.

JERRY *doesn't look up, concentrating on gluing together two tiny (and resistant) stanchions.* GRAHAM *sways.*

GRAHAM. Chris is our… technical king. While Neil majors in landscaping, and George here, has particular prowess in track-side buildings –

GEORGE. Yes! This, for instance, is a part of my own Nottingham Victoria Station display. 1903. I've been showing it for twenty years now, with fresh bits added each time round. It's a new ticket office this year! Of course, the philistines razed the station in the 1960s, built a shopping centre in its place – I mean, obviously, we have to live in the present but… why does it *always* have to be at the cost of destroying the past?

JORDAN. I…

(*To* GRAHAM.) Do I have to answer that now?

GRAHAM. No. It's… rhetorical –

JORDAN. Oh! Good –

(*Distracted.*) N-gauge! Now you're talkin'!!

He is pointing to JERRY *who doesn't react: ever more caught up in trying to glue the fiddly stanchions together…*

I love the intricate stuff. That's what I wanna try and move into meself!

GRAHAM. Ah, well, in which case, Jerry's the man to speak to. He's absolutely –

JERRY (*losing patience*). Fuck it…! Fucking fucking fuck it!

GRAHAM. – first class. In that regard.

JERRY. You… fucking… fuckers –

It becomes apparent JERRY*'s actually addressing his hands.*

NEIL. You okay there, Jerry?

An ashen GRAHAM *has locked eyes with* JORDAN.

GRAHAM. He's especially big on… innovation and…

JERRY. I fucking hate you!!

He balls his gnarled hands – as KEN *crosses, pats him.*

KEN. Hey! What's goin' on'?

JERRY. What? Oh. Nothing. Just… Few… technical issues –

JERRY *grabs his mug, he hesitates.*

Can someone… get me a drink, please? I… I've got a hell of thirst…

CHRIS *takes the mug.*

It's that smell. 'S… getting right to the back of my throat –

NEIL. The chilli con carne?

JORDAN. Mate, he means the propellant. I noticed that –

He sniffs.

It's Butanone… Methyl ethyl ketone. Probably mixed with dimethylformamide –

GRAHAM. He… studied chemistry –

CHRIS *offers* JERRY *some water.*

CHRIS. There you go, pal. You haven't seemed yourself all night… what's going on?

JERRY. Nothing!!

Sorry… Feel a bit… wobbly. I mean… I did take some pills –

GRAHAM. Pills??

JERRY. Painkillers. For my hands which… apparently… are getting arthritic. Just feel… fucking clumsy to me. Only… the medic, he said I needed 'em. And some diazepam as well, 'cause I get these spasms, in my neck –

KEN. Whoa! I'm had them! They can make you go dead funny –

JERRY. He said that! So… I got out in front of it. You know? Attack's the best form of defence. I always said that to my people, Jordan. Attack! Attack! Attack! And I organised some different pills –

(*To* GEORGE.) From that young man I used to mentor

He removes scrap of paper from his pocket.

– MDMA. Which he said'd counter the diazepam and make me feel like I was eighteen again –

JORDAN. It will do! He's give your friend ecstasy. Methylenedioxymethamphetamine. He's off his tits –

GRAHAM. What?!

JORDAN. There's tons of it round uni.

I did some Freshers' Week but it must'a come from a bad batch 'cause it made me shit meself in the night. Is everyone on drugs, Graham? Is that like… what you do before you get the trains out?

GRAHAM. No! He's… gone rogue. He –

(*To* NEIL.) We should get him home.

KEN. I'll do it –

JERRY. No. No. I wanna stay! If there might be… lavatory issues. And in any case, I can't let Anne see me… off my tits. She wouldn't recognise me!

Everyone looks to JORDAN.

JORDAN. He'll be fine. Honest.

(*To* JERRY.) Havin' said that, is Anne your wife? 'Cause they reckon mekkin' love when you're on E's bangin' so… you know, that might be a reason to get home.

JERRY *moans again, and his legs give.*

GRAHAM. He's staying! And… that's an end to it… We will contain the crisis and… move on –

He shifts JORDAN *out of the way with a rictus smile.*

To the test track. Let's take a look at that –

JORDAN. Actually, Graham, I'm alright. I've seen enough –

GRAHAM. But –

JORDAN. And me mate's waitin' in the car park –

GRAHAM. It's calmer in there! There *is* damp –

JORDAN. Besides which, I've already made me mind up –

GRAHAM. Please! We're good people –

JORDAN. And I definitely wanna join. It's fucking insane, man!

Thumping music starts to blast from the room speakers.

GRAHAM. What the –?

JORDAN. And you have tunes, 'n'all!? This is sick!!

GRAHAM. What's going on?

CHRIS. It's your wife!

GRAHAM. What?

KEN. It's Linda! She's in the kitchen!

Everyone is having to almost shout now.

JORDAN. You know what, Graham, you should put all this on the website. That there's drugs and music. You'd get loads more apply –

LINDA *appears – masked.* JORDAN *whoops.*

LINDA. I can't find the off button!

JORDAN *now pumps his hands in the air.*

KEN. What?

She realises she wears the mask still, and removes it.

LINDA. I can't find the off button –

KEN *dashes over, miming.*

KEN. You have to pull the plug out.

They hurry into the kitchen. JORDAN *turns to* GRAHAM.

JORDAN. Anyway… I *am* gonna make tracks. But like I say… this is brilliant!

(*Shouting to the others.*) People don't know, do they? Model railwayin'. They think it's borin'!!

He strides out. As the music stops. KEN *and* LINDA *reappear.*

LINDA. I am *so* sorry.

She beams. It was quite fun.

Who was that?

She looks to GRAHAM. He turns slowly back from staring at the door through which JORDAN has just left.

GRAHAM. *That* was Jordan. And he was here to… experience a typical club night.

LINDA *notes* GRAHAM*'s peculiar expression. As* JERRY *staggers upright.*

JERRY. Knew all about track dimensions. *And* satisfying your wife. Kid was a genius.

He slumps back onto his stool. LINDA*'s concern grows.*

LINDA. Are you alright, Jerry?

GRAHAM. No. He's not alright! He's taken an overdose of ecstasy.

(*Looks to* JERRY.) On a club night! We don't do ecstasy on club nights, Jerry. We're not that sort of a club!! Oh –

He turns, traumatised.

My God…

I *finally* get someone to express an interest in joining us and – not just anybody either! Somebody who isn't old and isn't white and… Somebody who is the model railwaying equivalent of a… fucking unicorn, and we put on a show like that!

GEORGE. But… Graham, it might have been touch and go for a moment, except he *does* want to join us.

GRAHAM. Only on the grounds that we're part hobby club, part crack den!!

GRAHAM *points to main door.*

How's he gonna feel next week? When he discovers that we *don't* normally solder to a backing track of Club Classics!!

(*To* LINDA.) I mean, really, what were you doing –

Now he jabs a finger at the speakers.

– what was that… unconscionable din?!

GRAHAM *stares. And his righteous indignation sends a surge of heat coursing through* LINDA'*s entire body.*

LINDA. *That* was Farley 'Jackmaster' Funk's 'Love Can't Turn Around'. Twelve-inch extended megamix.

GRAHAM. Mega what?

LINDA. I wanted to dance to it –

GRAHAM. Want –

LINDA. Yes! Graham. Dance. It's a hobby of mine. Like you build model railways, I like to dance. Only for a long time, I forgot that I did. Until I had a chat with Ken… some months ago, when we talked about music and the groups we liked – for which I thank you, Ken, for being interested in what I was interested in and… for making me feel… Well… rather less invisible, actually.

(*Back to* GRAHAM.) And that is what that music was!

She moves to the door. GRAHAM *steps after her.*

GRAHAM. Linda. You're being –

KEN. Who wants to see Woodcroft, then?

All eyes to KEN.

I've brought the layout in this evening and… It's more or less there, so…

(*Nods; then focuses on* LINDA *alone.*) I mean, I enjoyed it, too – when we talked, Linda, that night and…

It sort of… encouraged us to… just crack on and… get it done. So… *you* should have a look, especially. You all should. Before I let the public loose on it. Let me just –

He strides through the door.

GEORGE. Goodness. Goodness me! I haven't felt this excited since my wedding night!

NEIL (*doubtful*). Really?

GEORGE. Gwen and I had a hotel in Oakham. Right next to the station. And the honeymoon suite actually overlooks the signal box which is the one Airfix modelled their original Dublo on! I couldn't tear my eyes away…! Gwen did laugh –

He stops. KEN *is already back. He looks pale, drawn.*

KEN. Sorry. I… I forgot…

The water trough in't here and… that's… critical, you know. So, I will need… a little bit longer. Just to get it spot-on… Yeah. Just a… few more days and… I'll show it you then. When it's really ready… Properly.

Blackout.

'Rebel Rebel' by David Bowie.

Scene Five

The music fades…

KEN (*voiceover*). Careful…! Careful!! Bleedin' hell!

Lights up.

May 17th, 2019.

Wall-bars, cricket nets and basketball hoops, indicate a modern-day sports hall, at the centre of which we see the main Frodingham display and many other recognisable MDMRC efforts. Some commercial outlets have already erected their pitches, too. We notice trade banners hanging from the wall-bars, as well as a large ceiling hung one, announcing that this is 'The Stamford Model Railway Show, 2019'. A clock says, 9.30 p.m. KEN *and* JORDAN *enter carrying a sizable layout.* KEN *struggles to check a sheet of paper.*

KEN. Hang on… Yeah. It's right at the back. That one in the middle.

He leads them on and finally, they lay down the long display – covered still by a sheet.

There. That's it… Nice and easy… Good lad.

KEN steps back. Then he crosses and removes the sheet. The display is gorgeous. JORDAN stares, nods.

JORDAN. Nice. Nice one, Ken.

KEN. Yeah. I… It's alright –

(*Brusque.*) I'll wire up the transformers tomorrow.

Bring the rolling stock in then and… Bingo.

He crosses from the table. JORDAN remains, looking.

JORDAN. Hah!

JORDAN looks round. He follows KEN.

They're not gonna believe it when you tell 'em –

KEN. I'm not GONNA tell 'em!

JORDAN stops, lost.

'Cause they won't believe me even then. Or they'll… start askin' a load of questions so… they can have a nice surprise tomorrow, can't they. When they turn up first thing. Along with everyone else.

JORDAN. So are we still goin' for a pint, then? As per Graham's schedule: six till eight, get-in… eight till ten, The Danish Invader.

KEN. Can do. If you like… Or we can go and do summat on our own.

JORDAN. How'd you mean?

KEN. I dunno. Get a Chinese. My treat. Like a thank-you for helpin' me and… To say I'm pleased you joined the club; hope you enjoy your time with us, et cetera, et cetera – all that bollocks.

JORDAN. That'd be lovely, Ken. Especially when it's so heartfelt.

KEN. What you on about? I've just offered you a free Chinese – you mardy bastard!

JORDAN *smiles, gives the finger, and exits. KEN grins. Then he looks back at his display. His smile fades… He nods.*

Woodcroft.

He switches off the fluorescent tubes. He leaves. The clock hands move to quarter past four. Then a loud bang and a pair of fire doors fly open. Four FIGURES in jeans, trainers, and hoodies, step into the room. One carries a bottle of blue alcohol. They look at the displays. One of them moves to the front. Chris's Von Ryan carriage has pride of place there. The FIGURE picks it up. He holds it out, like an offering.

'Anarchy in the UK' by Sex Pistols. Loud.

He puts it on the floor.

As the first lyrics play, the figure stamps on the carriage. It shatters.

The other figures stalk towards the displays, as, just before the verse –

Blackout.

End of Act One.

ACT TWO

Scene One

May 18th, 2019

Lights snap on. The clock says 7.15 a.m. LINDA stands, shocked, in the middle of what is now, utter devastation. GRAHAM enters.

LINDA. What did they say?

GRAHAM. They've got CCTV. But it's not clear… They're leaving an officer on the gate. To turn all the other exhibitors away.

He crosses to a table with a few salvaged bits on it.

LINDA. You okay?

GRAHAM. I… I'm not sure, I…

I feel a bit peculiar… you know…

She crosses and takes his hand. He looks at her, adrift.

CHRIS (*offstage*). Graham!?

JERRY. We're here –

NEIL. We got the message –

JERRY, NEIL *and* CHRIS *have burst in. And stop, stunned.*

CHRIS. Jesus…

NEIL. They've… Everything. They… No. No! That's me Bassett-Lowke –

He crosses and picks up an engine's smashed carcass. CHRIS turns urgently towards his spot.

CHRIS. Where's Von Ryan? Where's –

He stops. He makes a noise. He crosses, too. He picks up the side of shattered carriage. He fights tears, looks away.

NEIL. But… Why would anyone – ? We're not hurting anybody. We're –

He looks to GRAHAM *and* JERRY*, imploringly.*

Why would anyone do this?

CHRIS. Who are they after?

LINDA. They don't know.

GRAHAM. But they are confident they'll get them… They know it was four people. And they're gonna go door to door. The estate round the back. The agricultural place up on the hill –

JERRY *groans, overcome. He steadies himself against the wall, trying to contain himself.*

Yours is okay, Jerry! I mean… Some of it. Look… here!

You'll be able to mend that.

JERRY. Absolutely. That's… key now… How we respond… It's not how often you get knocked down, it's –

CHRIS. Don't! Don't you fucking dare… I don't need one of your motivational quotes right now, Jerry, I really don't –

JERRY. I –

CHRIS. No!

CHRIS *gathers up the Von Ryan.*

If you had even the slightest idea of how human nature really works, you wouldn't've got booted out your own company for bein' such a fucking relic, would you?

LINDA. Chris – !

KEN (*offstage*). Lads! We –

KEN *and* JORDAN *run in. But they, too, stop, shocked.*

JORDAN. Bloody hell…

KEN. Who – ?

NEIL. They don't know.

JORDAN's attention has moved to the spot where they placed KEN's display the night before –

JORDAN. Oh, come on! That's taking the piss!

LINDA. What is it?

JORDAN. Woodcroft! They've… smashed up Woodcroft, Ken –

CHRIS. What do you mean… Woodcroft – ?

(*To* GRAHAM, *angry*). What's he talking about?

KEN's gaze snaps to CHRIS. He shuts up. GEORGE blunders in.

GEORGE. Men! I'm here. I –

He stops, eyes widen.

Oh… Oh, dear, it's… It's much worse than… Oh –

GEORGE collapses, legs gone. JORDAN manages to catch him –

JORDAN. Whoa –

LINDA. George – !

Get a chair. Quickly –

KEN helps JORDAN with GEORGE.

KEN. Good lad, I've got him. Down here, George. Here you go –

(*To* LINDA.) Can you fetch him a glass of water? And call the doc–

GEORGE. No! Just the water, please –

LINDA hurries out and GEORGE pats down his jacket.

Need my spray, for under my tongue –

CHRIS. Here. I'll get it. Hang on –

He removes a small spray bottle from GEORGE's jacket. GEORGE whimpers, opens his mouth. CHRIS sprays. Then GEORGE is distracted, pointing. He starts to get up.

GEORGE. Wait. That's – !

KEN. George! Just sit there a minute –

GEORGE. Victoria Station. Victoria Station's gone!

He totters over and picks up a ruined piece of his display. Then he looks urgently to a different area of the hall.

And Frodingham! It's… All of it – !

GRAHAM. No. No. Not all of yours, George! I found a piece –

GRAHAM *rushes to the table.*

A recognisable piece. Which you can repair. It's *all* repairable. You just need to spend some time and –

GEORGE. I don't *have* time! It took me twenty years, Graham. Twenty years and…

GEORGE *looks round at the total devastation.*

Time is the one thing I don't have.

He groans, sways, unsteadily, and KEN grabs him again.

KEN. Sod this! I'm gerrin him to the hospital –

GEORGE *protests.*

Whether you like it or not –

He starts to help GEORGE to the door. NEIL hurries across.

NEIL. I'll give you a hand –

KEN. Jerry… Can you tek Jordan back wi' you?

JERRY. Absolutely. Course. Roger that.

KEN, GEORGE *and* NEIL *leave.* JERRY *looks to JORDAN who stands to one side, clearly shaken.*

Got the MG with me, so… we can get the roof down and…
play some bangers –

His heart isn't in it.

– Whatever.

He shepherds JORDAN *out. Only* GRAHAM *and* CHRIS
remain. GRAHAM *sifts through the mess once more.*
CHRIS *stares.*

CHRIS. It won't be anyone from round here.

GRAHAM. What?

CHRIS. Done this. Be someone who doesn't respect our
traditions… Be an outsider.

He walks off. GRAHAM *watches the door slowly close –*

Blackout.

'Idiot Wind' by Bob Dylan.

Scene Two

Lights up.

May 24th, 2019.

We are back in the club room above the pub. LINDA *sits,
flicking through a sheaf of papers. The main table has a solitary
circle of track running around it. A lone locomotive clicks
across the rails. She looks increasingly frustrated by it. Finally,
she stands and removes the engine. She sits again.* GRAHAM
enters.

GRAHAM. Linda. There's another reporter downstairs. I'm
gonna deal with them before I come up –

He notices the empty track.

What happened to the train?

LINDA. It was irritating me.

GRAHAM *frowns, lost.*

I'll put it back when the boys arrive.

GRAHAM. Right. Good.

He crosses to the track, nods.

We will not let those vandals win. What we do here is too important –

He inhales. She looks at him. And barks a laugh. He turns.

LINDA. I'm sorry… It's just… what you do here is… Well, it's a hobby – in which you… recreate the world in miniature!

It's not… *important* at all in the usual sense of the word –

GRAHAM *is taken aback.*

GRAHAM. Linda –

LINDA. What *is* important – especially now you're so… clearly back to your old self again, is that you use this evening's meeting to tell everybody about the brewery's plans to throw you all out.

GRAHAM*'s eyes widen.*

Everything's already in so much flux, it would seem the perfect opportunity.

She looks directly at him. He takes a moment.

GRAHAM. Right… yes. I mean… I can see why you might think that but… another hammer blow, *so* soon. I –

GRAHAM *shakes his head.*

I'm not sure that's advisable. Though I will give it some thought, thank you.

He glances away, then back.

And meanwhile, I wonder whether you should get the oven on? I did promise hot food… exactly as if it were a regular club night.

He nods and hurries out. A moment and her jaw flexes. She looks upset. Then she hears raised voices coming up the stairs and ducks into the kitchen. CHRIS *and* NEIL *enter.*

NEIL. You're like a stuck record –

CHRIS. It's not me saying it. It's the police –

GEORGE *appears behind them, panting.*

GEORGE. Men. Men, please –

NEIL *looks like he's going to say more then remembers himself.*

NEIL. Yeah. Course. Sorry, George.

Come here –

NEIL *helps* GEORGE *out of his jacket and (grunting) into a chair.*

GEORGE. I know we're upset but… We should try and be civil… I *was* only allowed out on the grounds I avoid any stressful situations.

NEIL. No. No. We get that.

(*To* CHRIS.) Besides, it's not like it'll make any difference; finding out who's done it –

CHRIS. We know who's done it –

NEIL. We do not! Not until they arrest someone –

CHRIS. They've probably already left the country and gone home –

NEIL *groans – loudly.*

GEORGE. Actually, Chris –

CHRIS. The cops said: they were gonna make enquiries up at that farm camp.

NEIL. Amongst others –

CHRIS. Others?! The Fens're like a magnet this time of year… And alright, they're not all bad, I know that. I go quizzing with one bloke, Pavel, and he's good as gold. Comes here to pick and graft and send money home. But there's plenty of others who *have* got an axe to grind –

NEIL. With model railways?

CHRIS. With this country! 'Cause they're envious.

NEIL *turns.*

NEIL (*incredulous*). Jesus –

CHRIS. They are! They hate the fact we've got… democracy and… Shakespeare and… we drive on the left!

NEIL (*re-engaging*). How, in God's name –

CHRIS. Model railways are right at the heart of that!

GEORGE *can't see it.*

GEORGE. Really? I – ?

CHRIS. Think about it! What we do is quintessentially British! And not just as an hobby, 'cause of what it depicts – which is this nation's history in all its glory! And that is why our show got trashed.

CHRIS *points at* NEIL.

And he, and all his lefty mates who loathe everything that puts the Great into Britain, they've been fannin' the flames of discontent for years, and it's that which has given a bunch of jealous, spiteful scumbags the green light to get stuck in!

NEIL. You're… fuckin' insane –

CHRIS. And you know the biggest irony, Neil, as soon as you see *anybody* who isn't from these shores bein' proud of *their* country, you're the first to start clappin' and cooin' –

NEIL *makes to speak.*

It's a fact!

Every time there's someone on *Bake Off* who says they've drawn on their heritage to add a twist to the créme pat, you get a semi soft-on! Don't deny it! Yet when we proudly put a flag in our garden and start celebratin' everything that makes us, *us*, you turn your nose up! Why is that, do you reckon?

He leans closer.

It's 'cause you think it's only white-van man and a bunch of low-life rednecks who are proud of this country. Which means you're not only an hypocrite, you're a fuckin' snob, 'n'all!!

LINDA *re-appears, determinedly upbeat. She carries plates.*

LINDA. Evening! Evening, everyone.

GEORGE. Linda! Thank goodness.

LINDA. Graham'll be up in a minute. He's finishing an interview.

GEORGE. Just having you here makes me feel better!

CHRIS *points to a stack of cardboard boxes.*

CHRIS. You should take a look in those boxes of bits, George. That'll get the blood pressure pumpin' again –

NEIL. Why would you say that? To him?

LINDA *turns, sensing the atmosphere.* GRAHAM *enters.*

GRAHAM. Done! Finally!

He beams. GEORGE *tries to placate* CHRIS *and* NEIL.

GEORGE. The key thing's that we're together! It's a comfort –

GRAHAM *is straight to the helm.*

GRAHAM. Exactly. That's what the –

He points to the track.

Oh. You haven't put it back –

CHRIS. Who were you talking to?

GRAHAM. The *Peterborough Telegraph.* They'd picked up on a report in the *Stamford Mercury* –

NEIL (*to* GEORGE). I didn't know we were in there?

GRAHAM (*to* LINDA). I did try and get the reporter to sit in on club night… witness some of the… badinage. But she had to dash off suddenly.

LINDA. Did she?

GRAHAM. Needed to get over to the Conservative Club. Gauge reaction.

CHRIS. Why? What's happened?

LINDA. Theresa May's resigned.

NEIL (*to* CHRIS). You not seen? Bloody hell… Finally buggered by Brexit. I think that was the headline in the *Mail* –

GRAHAM. Gentlemen –

NEIL. Still, the way's clear for the blond twat now; you'll be pleased –

JERRY *enters with a walking stick.*

JERRY. Evening.

Everyone now stares at JERRY, *who looks bent and diminished.*

GRAHAM. Jerry. Have you… had an accident?

JERRY. No. I… I'm supposed to use it.

Just haven't bothered up to now. Then I thought… tonight. Why not?

GRAHAM. Of course…

GRAHAM *nods, uneasily, then turns, ready to make a start.*

GEORGE. Has anyone heard from Ken? I've rung several times and got no reply… I'm worried. I mean, at least the stuff we lost – the personal stuff – we'd exhibited before. Whereas Ken… he lost his entire life's work! He lost Woodcroft!!

CHRIS *is far too febrile to hear this.*

CHRIS. Did he though, George?

GEORGE. What?

CHRIS (*glances round*). Come on! I'm not the only one thinking it, am I?

GEORGE. I… don't understand. He left the layout in the hall. Jordan confirmed that –

CHRIS. Course he did! On pain of death. You know what Ken's like.

GRAHAM (*uneasy*). I –

CHRIS. I'm sorry, George, you're a man of God, you see the best in people – you can't help it. But it's obvious what's happened! Ken polled up, before anyone else, saw the mess and… realised he could use it.

NEIL. What do you mean: *use it*?!

CHRIS. By… goin' nuclear! He legs it back to his van, grabs the few raggedy-arsed bits of Woodcroft he has managed to finish – which in normal circumstances, he would've bottled showing at the eleventh hour – only *this* time, he drags it all out, lugs it into the hall and tips the whole lot in with the general devastation. Then, a quick tap dance on top and *bingo*! The whole sorry saga of the layout that will *never* be ready, is finally put to bed!

LINDA. Chris!

CHRIS. What? I'm right! Woodcroft's his… Waterloo!

It's where he's over-reached himself. How else do you explain all the secrecy around it, and the fact that no one's *ever* seen the entire layout? It's because he's embarrassed about it! 'Cause he knows, deep down, that… Woodcroft's a bit shit!!

GEORGE. Oh – !!

GEORGE *has heard enough. He stands.*

GRAHAM. Geeeeeorge, don't –

GEORGE. Don't what? Get upset?

GEORGE *pulls on his jacket.*

About the… the filth that spills from his mouth!

He crosses to the door.

CHRIS. Hang on. That's a bit –

GEORGE. Unreasonable!? It's not actually! Especially in the light of what has just happened to us in that gymnasium. Which is *shattering* if I'm honest… Except I *am* a man of God – you're right, which means I *won't* give in to my anger or to any feelings of… hatred or… bigotry – towards *anyone*!! But that does not mean it is easy! It is not! Which is why, I am going to go now, and call in at St Guthlac's and I am going to pray for you. To make peace with that thing inside you which causes you to be so… at war with… everyone! Because otherwise, I fear I may express what I actually feel about you, which is that you… you, Chris –

(*To* LINDA.) And this is not said in a pejorative sense, Linda; I've mentioned to Gwen, many a time, that her pudenda is a thing of wonder to me but in modern parlance it seems to bite, so –

(*To* CHRIS.) You are a complete and utter cunt!!

GEORGE *turns to the others.*

Good evening –

He throws open the door and strides out.

Arrgh!

He trips full-length over two Post Office sacks, which stand directly in front of the exit.

GRAHAM. George!

JORDAN (*offstage*). George!

The door swings shut as everyone rushes across.

GRAHAM. George. Are you alright?

GRAHAM *throws open the door again. We see* JORDAN *helping a jittery* GEORGE *back to his feet.*

JORDAN. I am *so* sorry –

GEORGE. Oh… Oh –

NEIL (*to* JORDAN, *censorial*). What are you doing?

JORDAN. I didn't know anyone was comin' out –

CHRIS. Here… Sit him down. George. Just here –

CHRIS *grabs a chair as* NEIL *shifts the bags.* JORDAN *leads* GEORGE *through. He helps him onto the proffered chair.*

JORDAN. Are you okay?

GEORGE. It's fine. I'm fine. Honestly –

JORDAN. I just –

GEORGE. Really –

GEORGE *rubs* JORDAN*'s shoulder.*

My dear boy… Don't worry. It was… the shock, that's all…! I'm completely unscathed!

He beams and JORDAN *looks mightily relieved. As* LINDA *turns back to the door, which is jammed open by one of the sacks.*

LINDA. So, Jordan, what *are* you doing?

JORDAN. I'm… clearin' downstairs!

In the tap room. Frank's gone ape!

JORDAN *looks at sacks.*

He reckons they're taking up too much space.

NEIL. What are they?

JORDAN. They're… the donations!

GRAHAM. What?

JORDAN. The appeal.

CHRIS. What appeal?

JORDAN (*exasperated*). The… 'get over havin' our entire club reduced to rubble' appeal!! Bloody hell! Has nobody looked at the socials? I stuck it up there. And a couple of model railwayin' sites piled on straightaway and we got a load of mentions and re-tweets from them and… I think we've just blown up basically.

JERRY. I don't really know what you're talking about. But it sounds positive.

JORDAN *beams: finally someone is striking the right note.*

JORDAN. It is! People are steppin' forward, Jerry! In a gesture of model railwaying solidarity. There's a couple of trackside buildings from France in there.

LINDA. No –

JORDAN. Honest! Plus a little lad from Leeds who's sent us ninety-five pence, which is his pocket money for the entire week –

GRAHAM. So… People have just… decided to help us? And it's resulted in all that –

He points to the sacks and then looks to JORDAN *again.*

JORDAN. Well, no. It hasn't resulted in all that. There's eight more sacks downstairs. I just an't had a chance to bring 'em up yet.

The oldsters straighten – stunned.

Blackout.

Scene Three

'Theme From S-Express' by S-Express.

Lights up.

June 7th, 2019

The edges of the room are cluttered with even more Post Office bags and donated scenery, as well as stacks of cards. It's hot. JERRY, CHRIS and LINDA fan themselves. GRAHAM and NEIL check kit.

NEIL. What's that?

GRAHAM. Oh, it's a… I'm not quite… It's not a Wrenn, is it?

NEIL. It can't be. Surely –

   NEIL and GRAHAM lean in, sigh.

GRAHAM. No. No. It's… I dunno what it is. But it's lovely. It… hasn't got an engine.

   He places the bogie in a big box on the side marked 'DUDS'.

NEIL. We can still use the body –

GRAHAM. And they sent a couple of baseboards, too, so… Can't expect them all to be winners! I think Jerry's been especially blessed. In the N-gauge! Eh, Jerry?… Are you not on with those tonight?

JERRY. Yeah. I just…

   He indicates large scale tender.

I saw some O which looked… quite interesting –

LINDA. Goodness me. Fifty pounds.

GRAHAM. No!

   LINDA waves cheque and reads a card.

LINDA. 'With you in your hour of need.'

GRAHAM. Can you send them a special thank-you…? Ha!
I can't quite believe it!

LINDA *reads a different card.*

LINDA. This one says: 'Here's a fiver, bring back the birch…'
Looks like the same handwriting as that bloke who sent us
an address for tasers on the dark web…

GRAHAM. Right. Well. Maybe just take the cash there and…
let the police have a look at the card.

He scoffs.

Who knew that model railwayers were such… passionate
people?!

That's almost five hundred quid now!

He crosses, grabs another box of donated items. LINDA
watches.

LINDA. Quite bittersweet though, I imagine.

GRAHAM *looks back.*

So much of what's been destroyed is custom-made, isn't it?

You can't just wander into a modelling shop and buy
a replacement off the shelf.

CHRIS. Hear, hear!

He nods as he cleans a crayoned carriage.

And that's why the culprits have to be caught and held to
account! As ye sow, so shall ye reap. That's the British way.

GRAHAM. I think that's Galatians, isn't?

CHRIS. Is it…? The point being, it *was*… a devastating attack,
Linda, and money *can't* provide all the answers. Which is
where… justice softens the blow. I mean, I keep thinking
about me Von Ryan, in that respect. Same as his Bassett-
Lowke –

CHRIS *points to* NEIL.

Was seven years, wannit? You'd been rebuilding that? And then it's just… gone and… it's like –

CHRIS *shrugs.*

(*To* LINDA.) – all that care you put into it and… All the… love, really… You'll never get it back. Ever.

NEIL *sees* CHRIS*'s genuine pain and feels conflicted.*

NEIL. But just wantin' to see people punished for it, though – it in't gonna… *change* anything so… I just think the best you can do is… be grateful for the kindnesses folk *are* showin' and… try and move on. How Graham says.

LINDA. Actually, if you want to *fully* recover from trauma, apparently, *the* most critical thing to do is acknowledge *all* of the feelings it arouses in you –

She looks to busy GRAHAM.

You don't just blithely pick up again as if nothing's happened –

JORDAN *enters.* LINDA *stands instantly.*

Jordan! How'd you get on?

GEORGE *shuffles in, too.* JORDAN *turns to help him.*

GEORGE. No sign.

JORDAN *eases* GEORGE *into a chair. He sits with a grunt.*

JORDAN. We rang his bell and tapped on the window but…

He shakes his head.

GEORGE. In the end, I shoved a note through the door: 'Dear Ken, how are you? We'd love to see you back at club nights' –

He looks to GRAHAM.

That's almost three weeks now, Graham! With zero contact!

GRAHAM *looks uneasy – he doesn't want his parade rained on. A muffled phone rings and everyone looks round.*

JORDAN. 'S alright. It's mine –

He roots around in his messenger bag. Eventually he checks his phone.

It's the *Mercury*… That reporter –

He answers the phone.

Hello… Yeah, it is… What? When?

The others all straighten, hearing his tone.

Have they said –

JORDAN *looks to the others.*

Right. Right… I see… Sure… No! You better speak to the chairman –

He holds out the phone to GRAHAM.

They've caught 'em. The people who trashed the show. The cops've got 'em –

CHRIS *steps closer.*

CHRIS. Who was it?

GRAHAM *grabs the phone.*

GRAHAM. Hello… Yes, it is –

JORDAN (*to* LINDA). She wanted a comment –

CHRIS. Bollocks to comments. Who did it?!

GRAHAM *raises his voice.*

GRAHAM. Sorry. I –

He looks across at the others.

I can't hear you. Just… give me a second –

He passes outside for privacy. JORDAN *watches him go.*

CHRIS. Jordan!!

JORDAN *finally turns back.*

JORDAN. The're local. School kids.

CHRIS. What?

JORDAN (*to* GEORGE). They only live up the road. They were out before their GCSEs, got bevved up and went nuts.

CHRIS. No. That's –

JORDAN (*to* LINDA). They didn't even know there was an exhibition on. They just… broke in the gym for a game of footy and… when they saw what *was* in there, they decided they'd go ahead…

(*To* JERRY.) Only without the ball.

A beat as everyone tries to compute this.

JERRY. But –

GEORGE. Why would you…?

NEIL. The li-ttle shits!!

They struggle to make sense once more. But then CHRIS *turns urgently to* JORDAN.

CHRIS. Are they down the station?

JORDAN. I… dunno –

CHRIS *nods.*

They'll be in the cells or… bein' processed. Who's coming?!

JERRY. What??

CHRIS. The cop shop! Who's coming with me?

LINDA. Why??

CHRIS. To… look 'em in the eye –

NEIL. What good's that gonna do?

CHRIS. I don't care! I… I just want to see 'em! And I want them to see me… Seein' 'em!!

He storms out, crossing GRAHAM, *who is hanging up his call. He frowns as he walks back into the room.*

GRAHAM. Where's he going??

GEORGE. The police station.

GRAHAM. Why?

NEIL. Exactly.

GRAHAM *hands* JORDAN *his phone back.*

GRAHAM. God. What a mess!

LINDA. And they just… stumbled across it.

NEIL. That makes it feel… even *more* wasteful! I'm not sayin' I'd rather it was lads who had a pathological dislike of train sets. Or maybe I am. I –

'Chooo choo!' Graham's phone this time. He groans, crosses to his bench and picks up his mobile. He looks at the number.

GRAHAM. Bet it's another reporter… It'll be non-stop now, you see.

He answers his phone.

Hello. Who is this, please?

He listens, straightens.

Sorry. I… could you repeat that?

His eyes widen and he waves frantically to the others. LINDA *shakes her head: 'What?' He quickly mouths two words back.*

LINDA (*quietly*). Who?

GRAHAM. Gosh… Really. Well, it's great to hear from you –

He looks wildly back. And hysterically re-mouths the words.

GEORGE. What's he saying?

GRAHAM*'s eyes widen further. He mimes frantically jabbing something up and down in front of him.*

I think that's self-pleasuring, isn't it?

LINDA. No. I don't think it's that, George –

GRAHAM *stops and laughs manically.*

GRAHAM. Right! Right!

He does the up-and-down stabbing: quicker and more forcefully.

JORDAN. To be fair, Linda –

LINDA. He isn't!!

GRAHAM. Really?!?!

They all look to GRAHAM *– to the new level of shock.* JERRY *holds his hands wide. 'GIVE US MORE!'* GRAHAM *thinks, repeats the gesture, adds a circular motion and then mimes propelling a fist towards his nether regions.*

NEIL. Summat about one in the bollocks but beyond that –

GRAHAM *stares, appalled. Then, he concentrates on the call.*

GRAHAM. No. No. We'd be delighted! Would you like a sweatshirt? Right. I'll get one sorted… Of course. And… thank you. Again!

He hangs up. He stares at the phone. The others wait…

LINDA. So?!

GRAHAM (*exasperated*). Rod Stewart!

GEORGE. What?

GRAHAM *does the stabbing mime.*

GRAHAM. Rod! As in drains –

The stirring one.

Stew! As in stirring of –

The whack in pubic area.

And hurt –

NEIL. As in one in the bollocks. I got that one! I said, didn't I?

He beams at the others. But LINDA *has moved on.*

LINDA. Rod Stewart – was on the phone to you??

GRAHAM *gets back on track – and nods.*

GRAHAM. Yes.

LINDA. Are you sure?

GRAHAM. What?

LINDA. Are you sure it was him?

GRAHAM. I – ?

A hoax had never occurred. He blinks, anxiously.

NEIL. Did he sing for you?

GRAHAM. No… I mean… It sounded like him. When I've heard him –

JERRY. You probably should have asked for a tune, skip. Just –

GRAHAM. It was him! It was… Rod! He *is* an enthusiast! A model railway enthusiast. I know that.

JORDAN. And Rod Stewart – he's a singer, is he?

The oldsters all look at JORDAN. GRAHAM mutters.

GRAHAM. Oh, God…

LINDA. What did he want?

GRAHAM. To help us! He'd read about our predicament and… he wants to make a donation. In return, we're sending him a sweatshirt; sizing to be confirmed later when I speak to his manager.

JORDAN. Nice one! How much is he chippin' in? Did he get into specifics?

GRAHAM. Oh, yes. Ten thousand pounds.

NEIL. What?

GRAHAM. Ten thousand. Just to get us back on our feet.

GEORGE. Fuck me!

Blackout.

Scene Four

'Baby Jane' by Rod Stewart.

Lights up.

July 1st, 2019.

GRAHAM *enters, humming, carrying a large box. He places it on the round table. In so doing, he reveals his T-shirt: emblazoned with Rod Stewart's face. He crosses to his phone and ups the volume on the track. He does a little dance move. He unpacks donations.* LINDA *appears – watches him.*

LINDA. Graham… Graham!!

GRAHAM. Sorry! Sorry –

> *He crosses to his phone and mutes the music.*

> Got carried away! One of my favourites. Course everybody loves that one.

LINDA. Right.

> *He transfers sections of track.* LINDA *watches him.*

GRAHAM. Did you know, by the way, that when he tours, Sir Rod books a second suite where he sets up his layout? And then, at the end of a gig it's just waiting there for him – so he can kick back and relax!

LINDA. I suppose you get bored of the cocaine and the blow jobs.

GRAHAM. Pardon?

> *He turns to face her – not sure he heard correctly.*

LINDA. I'm going round to Ken's. He's definitely at home. He just won't come to the door. So I'm going to try and speak to him – through the letterbox…

> GRAHAM *seems unsure.*

> He needs a human presence.

> *She crosses. Checks items on the 'trunk' table.*

GRAHAM. Fine. If you feel you want to. Then go ahead.

LINDA. I'm not asking for your permission. I'm telling you…

Now she searches counter.

I'm surprised you haven't been yourself, actually. It is trains, after all. You can do trains –

GRAHAM. Linda –

LINDA. I will be back, though. For the monthly committee meeting. I'm going to tell everyone about the eviction notice. And the need to vacate the premises –

GRAHAM. What?!

LINDA. You're obviously not going to –

GRAHAM. But… I'm chairman –

LINDA. Then grow a pair and step up!

She finds the notebook she was looking for, grabs it, and strides towards the door. He watches her and then, sharply:

GRAHAM. Linda!!

She turns. He never raises his voice. He blinks.

Why are you being like this?

She hesitates – but realises she's already started.

LINDA. Because of him.

She points at T-shirt.

Rod… bloody Stewart. And the way he's lit up your life!!

GRAHAM *is no clearer. It makes her smile – bitterly. Then:*

I am always on the *outside* of your world, Graham –

GRAHAM. I've told you, if you want to model –

LINDA. I –

She stops, calms herself, and begins again; needs to be clear.

That first weekend, when the vandalism happened, you actually started to talk to me. About your feelings…

Alright, there was a strong railway bias to everything but… you spoke *to* me and *I* was a part of you… The way we used to be –

GRAHAM. That's… nonsense! We were… exactly how we've always been! We're *not* the most… voluble… life-and-soul-of-the-party couple. But that's not our way. We're steady. We take quiet pleasure in the world – and in each other!

She stares at him. Sees she has to go in harder.

LINDA. Do you remember Fran?

He strains, then looks pleased.

GRAHAM. Yes. She was one of your hiking friends. From when you used to go off rambling all the time.

LINDA. We only ever went once. We climbed up Mam Tor.

GRAHAM. But… you were always away. In school holidays and… Whenever I was exhibiting.

LINDA. We were at Greenham.

GRAHAM. Sorry?

LINDA. Greenham Common. The women's peace camp. Easter '92 was the first time.

GRAHAM. No, that… That was… Scafell. Easter '92. You went up Scafell Pike and we won Three Counties at Lincoln. Seaton Viaduct in the Age of Steam.

LINDA. Yellow gate.

Which turned out to be a bit've a party gate, actually but… The women were wonderful! So welcoming.

He's about to speak when something new strikes him.

GRAHAM. Hang on… You took Jonathan. Several times. I had to buy him special boots –

LINDA. Well, it could be very muddy. He was such a good boy, too. I made him promise it was our secret – the thing Mummy liked to do, the way Daddy liked his railways and… he thought it was brilliant. There were loads of kids there.

She smiles. GRAHAM spins – any anger is already gone. Now he senses danger…

GRAHAM. Why didn't you tell me?

She looks. Knows what awaits him. And drives herself on.

LINDA. Because… whilst I believed in *everything* the camp stood for *and* what it was trying to achieve, I knew that I went there above all… because it thrilled me. It gave me purpose and put passion back into my life.

GRAHAM *sways. His mouth moves. Nothing comes out.*

I'm sorry, Graham. But… by then… I'd already become this… background presence to you. Like a heartbeat – essential but… not usually acknowledged –

GRAHAM. That's –

LINDA. Except it wasn't… *all* your fault! I see that now. *I* allowed the flame to whiten into ash, whatever else you were doing –

GRAHAM (*angry, despairing*). What… flame – ?

LINDA. The eternal flame! On our honeymoon in Bath. There was some graffiti on the Spa wall – fourth-century graffiti, and it said: 'The eternal flame shall *never* whiten into ash.'

LINDA *remembers, she nods.*

We squeezed hands when we read that. We never looked at each other but I remember we both squeezed hands…

She looks right at him.

And that passion's still in you, Graham.

I see it; around the vandalism… Sir Rod! Bringing Jordan on board –

LINDA *beams, then stops.*

Only it doesn't include me. And… I've had enough of it. Because I won't be shunted off, with all the other old people, down some… forgotten-about siding, to creak and go cold.

I intend to carry on, full pelt, to the very end of the line, so the question is, Graham, am I going to do it alone… or with the man I first got coupled to, all those years ago!

She looks at him, then kisses him on the lips. She steps back. He is stunned. Then he kisses her. Hard – almost without thought, pulling her into a passionate embrace. They separate, astonished. As NEIL bursts in.

NEIL. Graham…! Linda. Sorry. I – ?

GRAHAM. Please. Don't be we… We were –

LINDA. What is it? What's the matter?

NEIL. It's George.

Blackout.

Scene Five

'Forever Young' by Bob Dylan.

Lights up.

July 23rd, 2019.

The room is stuffed with donations. JERRY limps in using his stick. Then comes NEIL. And JORDAN. They are all in suit and black ties, all dragging mail sacks. LINDA walks in from the side room. She is dressed in funeral wear, too.

LINDA. More?

GRAHAM *enters next. Carrying a box. He places the box down, to wedge open the door and then goes to get another sack.*

I thought you said it was slowing down.

GRAHAM. I thought it was! Only then it started up again.
I mentioned it to that bloke from Al Jazeera –

NEIL. Al Jazeera?

GRAHAM. Apparently model railwaying's massive in the Middle East.

Music starts to flood up from the bar below. 'Da Ya Think I'm Sexy?' by Rod Stewart.

LINDA. Oh, God. Not that again! Has Frank got it on repeat or something?

NEIL. He has actually, yeah –

NEIL *closes the door.*

He leaked a story to the press that Rod'd flown over to see us – compare locos and that – and he had a cheese ploughman's downstairs. He's put a plaque above the salad cream.

GRAHAM. Right, well… Let's try and ignore it and… Make a start, I suppose –

NEIL. Should we though, Graham? Today?

GRAHAM. It's in his will! That's what Gwen said. Finger buffet, then back here to run all of our favourite stock. Victoria Station having pride of place.

They all shift. One piece of Victoria Station stands on the table.

I do wish he hadn't had to endure that… Right at the end of his life –

JORDAN. At the same time, Graham, George was the most positive out of any of us.

GRAHAM. No. You're right. He was. I thought that came across very well in the service.

LINDA. And how kind he was.

NEIL. It's true, though, innit?! I don't think George had a bad word for anyone.

JERRY. He called Chris a cunt.

NEIL. Apart from that…

    NEIL *chuckles.*

    And he loved this place. Dinni? Even with the mould and
    the… cold.

GRAHAM. Yes. Well, we're all finished here. So. It really *is*
    the end of an era.

NEIL. What?!

LINDA. What…?

GRAHAM. The brewery want us out.

    They're gonna convert the space into flats and… we have to
    find new premises.

JERRY. Now?! While we're still… reeling from the
    vandalism –

GRAHAM. Actually, Jerry, they told us ages ago. Last year,
    in fact. And Linda tried to get me to say something but…
    I didn't. And… I'd like to apologise to all of you. Especially
    to Linda… for not –

    Makes a squeezing gesture with both hands.

JORDAN. Milking a cow?

GRAHAM. Grasping the nettle! Which, going forwards,
    I intend to address – by devolving future key decisions
    much more to the membership. And in the spirit of that, and
    particularly in the light of George and his relationship to this
    place, I wonder what people think about naming our new
    club house after him?! So he literally leads us into the future.

LINDA. I think that's a lovely idea.

JERRY. Where, though? Where are we going?

GRAHAM. I don't know! I… I haven't really looked into it yet.
    But we should be able to find *somewhere* close. I mean, we
    can probably afford to pay a bit more rent now. What is the
    donation total currently, Linda?

LINDA. A hundred and twenty-five thousand pounds and sixty-three pence.

GRAHAM. Well, that should get us…

Something half-decent –

JORDAN. You're telling me!

JORDAN *steps forward, excited and looks to the others.*

GRAHAM. There was another thing. That I'd like some feedback on… I've increasingly had this feeling… which became a conviction, as I watched them lowering George into the ground this afternoon… that while all this –

He points to the boxes of kit on the side.

– represents an outpouring of staggering generosity… it's not us. *We* are the kit we were working on before the show. And it's *that* we should be putting all of our efforts into now: the old kit! The broken kit! The MDMRC kit!!

JORDAN *punches the air.*

JORDAN. Fuckin' get in there!!

NEIL. Are you serious? 'Cause I hadn't dare say anything, in case I seemed ungrateful but… if you are, then –

Goes to box marked: 'EXHIBITION DEBRIS', roots inside and emerges with more pieces of Victoria Station. He lays them beside the one standing bit.

We can fix that! We can fix all of it!

JORDAN. Cooooome on!

JORDAN *runs and roots in the box, too.*

This is like being in *Top Gun*! The bit where they all stride across the tarmac and jump in the jets! Come on, Jerry! Get yours out. The N Gauge; that's me favourite!

JERRY. Actually, Jordan, I'm thinking of taking a break from that.

NEIL, LINDA *and* GRAHAM. Jerry!? No. You –

JERRY. I just… feel that personally, I've gone as far as I can with the small scale and… I need a new challenge.

He quickly looks away. As the door flies open. CHRIS *bursts in, waving some paper.*

CHRIS. August the 19th! 10 a.m.!

NEIL. What?

CHRIS. The trial!! Judgement Day. Sword of Damocles. Schwishhh –

He gleefully makes a cutting gesture across his throat. Then he pulls off his jacket. He too wears a Rod Stewart T-shirt. Which he suddenly realises is very out of character.

Hang on… Why're you – ? Oh, no –

He looks at his watch.

No. I… I've been so caught up –

GRAHAM. July 23rd, 3 p.m.

CHRIS. I know! I just… Oh, shit! I feel terrible now… How was it? How did it go?

NEIL *hesitates; then:*

NEIL. It was lovely.

LINDA. Very George.

JERRY. That said, I still sat through most of it thinking it wasn't really happening. I got so used to him *nearly* dying…

CHRIS. Well… I'm glad. It went well and… I suppose in some ways, it's quite appropriate this's come through today, 'cause… this'll be the moment where justice gets served, won't it, and all our traditional values get restated. Everything George stood for.

LINDA. I think he stood for forgiveness more than anything, didn't he?

CHRIS *stares, then he scoffs awkwardly. Then he crosses and pins the sheet on the notice board.*

CHRIS. Either way, it's good it's finally gonna get settled. I think we can all agree on that. So we can move on… That's the point Boris was just mekkin. Outside Number Ten.

NEIL. Boris?

CHRIS. He's in. He's the new leader. And he's gonna Get Brexit Done. It's the first thing he said. Then *we* can move on, as a nation – which is what we're all cryin' out for. And he understands that! 'Cause he's one of us!!

They stare, agog. As the doors open and KEN *steps in.*

LINDA. Ken! Where have you been?! We –

She notes his suit.

Were you at the service?

KEN *shrugs awkwardly.*

KEN. I couldn't not pay me respects.

LINDA. Of course. I'm glad; you managed to make it.

There's an uneasy pause. JORDAN *crashes through it.*

JORDAN. Did you not get my emails?

KEN. I… I just needed some time, mate…

Another moment of tension which GRAHAM *feels. And breaks, by moving across to* KEN, *smiling positively.*

GRAHAM. Well, you're here now! That's the main thing. We were actually –

KEN. I'm not stopping. I've just come to say: I'm leavin' the club.

A further flurry of voices, of 'What?' and 'No!'

NEIL. You can't. If we've done summat wrong –

KEN. You haven't done anything!

He realises he's come in hard and dials it down at once.

I just… Since the show got smashed up and.Woodcroft went, I – Which, I know, might seem selfish 'cause you're all mangin' to carry on wi' what you lost except… I'm not and… that's it, basically.

He looks at them, drained. CHRIS *stares, trembles. And then.*

CHRIS. Only you didn't lose it, did you, Ken? Woodcroft *wasn't* destroyed by the vandals 'cause… you trashed it yourself.

KEN. What you talkin' about?

LINDA. Chris –

CHRIS. No, Linda. Enough's enough! This is for his own good –

GRAHAM. It's just a… theory he has, Ken –

CHRIS. Christ, you lecture me, about forgiveness. I'm trying to get him to forgive himself!

KEN. Forgive…?

CHRIS. Yeah, and we do forgive you, Ken! This is what I'm tryin' to say… We support you. Alright, you bit off more than you could chew wi' Woodcroft and… you knew, it didn't cut the mustard – so you took drastic action to get out the corner you'd backed yourself into… That's human nature, mate. It is NOT a resigning matter.

KEN. *You* think I smashed up me own layout, to cover the fact… I was ashamed of it?

CHRIS *smiles sadly. Then opens his arms to* KEN.

You miserable –

CHRIS. Arrgh –

KEN. Fuckin' –

KEN *grabs* CHRIS *by the scruff of his shirt and shoves him backwards. They hit the sofa and collapse over its arm. The rest of the lads try to split them up, shouting at* KEN *to leave* CHRIS, *even as* KEN *tries to throttle him.*

You bastard – !

ALL. Let him go! Get off him!

CHRIS. Urrgh –

LINDA. Ken!

KEN. I'll… rip your fuckin'– Arrrrgh!

The rest finally yank KEN off, and back across the room. He pants and tries to get free. JORDAN is appalled and scared.

JORDAN. Don't, Ken! You're gonna kill him –

This seems to inflame KEN further, and he roars, almost breaking clear. The lads struggle and CHRIS whimpers.

LINDA. Stop it! Stop it!! That is enough!

Her voice cuts through and finally KEN relents, panting.

We are the Market Deeping Model Railway Club. Not the Fight Club! So everybody, please, just… calm down…

JORDAN groans, on guard.

Especially you, Jordan… No one is killing anyone –

JORDAN. He might, though, Linda. He's stiffed someone before, anni!

It's like a gun has been fired. Everyone looks at JORDAN. And finally, KEN scoffs.

KEN. Is that what they told you? That I killed somebody? When I was in the army?

GRAHAM. We… That's –

KEN. How long did it tek 'em? Before they said summat. Was it the first week?

JORDAN. I think it was the second.

LINDA. Ken, nobody really –

KEN. No, it's true, Linda. I did… I killed five people, actually.

JERRY. Ken –

KEN (*to* JORDAN). Would you like to know what happened?

NEIL. Mate, c'mon –

KEN. Shuddup! I'm havin' a conversation. With one of the few people in this club who's actually honest with me. Him and Linda… So, *would* you, Jordan? Would you like to know?

JORDAN *stares. He nods.* KEN *smiles, nods, too. Thank you.*

I was an infantryman, in the Welsh Guards. We were at war, down in the Falklands. Sapper Hill… These Argies were dug in there and… They had our whole platoon pinned down. But only 'cause no one'd got a good look at 'em. 'Cept I could see, right away, three main positions, one next to the other, in a straight line. Which meant they were conscripts 'cause you never do that. You always set up in a curve, so you can fire across one another, give cover. Like they were… You can just get picked off from one end. So I did… I started with the first and worked me way down the line: bam, bam, bam; couple of grenades, me rifle. It was daft. Killin' people that easy…

He stalls. Nods. Carries on.

Then I got to the last trench and I shot the lad there who was on the machine gun – Browning M2 – that was what was causin' all the damage, only his mate'd seen me comin' by then and he turned on me and fired with a pistol. Point blank. But he missed me, so – I just threw meself on him and… I had me hands round his throat and we were wrestlin' on the floor and punchin' and… I bit his nose. I remember that… 'Cause all the iron, that's in your blood, I suddenly tasted that and I was scrabbling for me knife and… And then I realised: he was already dead. He'd been dead ages. Even while I'd been thumpin' him and… I'd stabbed him in the neck – just under his ear. Only, I couldn't remember doin' it and –

He starts to cry. It's horrible, pained. He fights it and finally stops enough to carry on.

And then… The strangest thing, as I was layin' there, right on top of him, I suddenly thought…

I know that aftershave… It was Aramis! Which is what I used to put on, when we were going out in Nottingham and we walked through Boots to get to the pub and we used to raid all the testers and… me and this lad I'd just –

He makes a jabbing motion, as if with a knife and suddenly he screws up his face. And he sobs again. It's worse. But he manages to stop himself more quickly. Then he looks to CHRIS. *He inhales, deeply.*

Woodcroft Station is where me dad got off the train to see me mum. When they started courtin'. He was in the RAF. The guards office had this old Pianola in it – My mum took me once – and there was a pen at one end of the platform where they used to keep the sheep before they got loaded up and sent off to market and… It's where me dad come in at the end of the war. And all the station staff were waitin' with me mum and they'd put all these Union Jacks out 'cause… He *was* a fucking hero –

He grits teeth, nods.

That's what that layout was. And I started it 'cause this doctor'd said I should find something, a hobby, which… took me somewhere… good. Where I felt calm and… 'Cause when I come out the army, I –

He shakes his head.

Anyway, it worked! Like nothin' else has been able to; which is why I was always scared, that when I finished it… I might, you know… not have that thing which kept me on an even keel, and I might –

He stops. Imagines. But then he beams – at LINDA.

Till you and me got talkin' about music, Linda, and…

I dunno, I just felt… joy. I can't put it no better than that. And… I thought: 'Stop bein' such a twat! And… get on with it…'

He smiles at LINDA *again.*

And I finished it. And it was perfect! Wan't it, Jordan? It was perfect. Only… now it's not. Now it's gone and –

He stops, frowns.

That's why I have to leave the club 'cause… I feel less certain about… *not* bein' how I can sometimes be and… *that* bloke, you don't want around. That bloke –

He shakes his head urgently.

He does bad shit, you know? He does shit like this.

He looks to CHRIS *and around the room, to indicate what's just happened. He leaves.* GRAHAM *faces* LINDA.

GRAHAM. What shall I do?

For a second she stares at GRAHAM, *amazed. Then.*

LINDA. Stay here. I'll talk to him… Ken! Ken, wait –

She runs out. There is a beat. The men look to each other.

JERRY. Christ…

JORDAN. That was my fault. I –

GRAHAM. You did nothing wrong-

JORDAN. Bu–

NEIL *(to* CHRIS*)*. It was *his* fault –

CHRIS. What? I only said what you lot were too scared to –

NEIL. Jesus…! George was bang-on about you –

CHRIS. I'm a cunt?

NEIL. No! You're at war… with *everyone*! You've had your
    fair share of crap, I get that: your missus and the Nespresso
    man, your uncaring, ingrate of a son, the demise of Von
    Ryan! But *always* tryin' to find someone to blame for it; it
    achieves nothing, Chris, *and* it just makes you feel ten times
    worse 'cause it's nonsense, you… stupid… racist, twat!

CHRIS *trembles, and storms out, the door wedging open.*

'The First Cut is the Deepest' by Rod Stewart, floods into the room.

GRAHAM. Right-oh.

GRAHAM *crosses and closes the door. He turns back.*

NEIL. I –

GRAHAM. No! You simply told the truth.

JERRY. Christ, what a debacle… Those bloody kids… and we'll never know why they did it.

JORDAN. No. We do know.

GRAHAM. What?

JORDAN. Why they did it.

JORDAN *slows, he looks worried.*

Why are you lookin' at me like that – ?

JERRY. Tell us.

GRAHAM. Yes, tell us, Jordan. Why did they do it?

JORDAN. Well… Because they're young. Which is a feeling you blokes are no longer familiar with. That's why you're all obsessed with the past in your layouts, 'cause the past is largely what your lives consist of now. Whereas those lads, they have the present and a vast and unclaimed land ahead of them, which is the future. *And* they still struggle to pee in the mornings thanks to the stirring and rock-hard erections they wake with… In other words, the reason they trashed our show, ultimately, is 'cause they could, and in the moment, it felt bloody brilliant.

A beat. JERRY *whimpers and slumps onto a chair. As* LINDA *strides in and stops.* GRAHAM *spins to the door.*

LINDA. What happened!? Chris just ran out saying he was gonna join Northcott, Overton and Barrowby –

GRAHAM. NOB!?

JORDAN. What about Ken?

LINDA. I persuaded him to stay. Have a drink… A Maggie
May Burger… I said he should come back up when he's
ready…

NEIL (*nods*). We'll look after him. That's why we're a club and
we don't all just model at home. Because we support each
other.

LINDA. I also told him about the plans to resurrect the smashed
kit, and I suggested that perhaps alongside Victoria Station,
we could prioritise *his* layout?

GRAHAM. Yes! Yes, that's brilliant –

LINDA. And maybe with *all* of the rebuilding you should work
jointly?

JORDAN. Yes! That as well! That's bang-on, Linda 'cause
a) it'll be more fun and b) it means you and me *can* model
together, Jerry, on the small-scale stuff –

JERRY *tries to speak.*

No! You can't bail now. I'm gonna be your apprentice.

JERRY *is stunned.*

Which reminds me: there's no need to worry 'bout your
hands. I'll do all the fiddly stuff and all you'll have to do is
point! Plus, I can get drugs if you need 'em. The main thing
is: I'm ready to learn!

JERRY (*still stunned*). From me?

JORDAN. Yes! Bloody hell, Jerry! It's not difficult. I wanna
model small. And you're Jerry Big Bollocks, King of the N
Gauge! Now bring it in!

JORDAN *holds his arms wide and* JERRY *steps into his
embrace, eyes filling. A second later though, he straightens*

and focuses on the door. As everyone does... KEN is there, unsure. GRAHAM walks towards him. He stops. The others join GRAHAM and finally KEN goes to them. They surround him. They talk.

Music up: 'Angel' by Rod Stewart.

Lights fade. Gauze in.

THEN, PROJECTED:

'ON 19th AUGUST 2019, FOUR LOCAL YOUTHS WERE FOUND GUILTY OF VANDALISING THE MARKET DEEPING MODEL RAILWAY CLUB ANNUAL SHOW AND CAUSING £60,000 OF DAMAGE.'

Card fades. Another comes up.

'THEIR PARENTS WERE EACH ORDERED TO PAY £500 COMPENSATION WHILE THE YOUTHS WERE SENTENCED TO COMMUNITY SERVICE ORDERS AND MADE TO WRITE A FORMAL LETTER OF APOLOGY.'

Card fades. Another one comes up:

'TO DATE, THE CLUB HAS RECEIVED MORE THAN £130,000 IN DONATIONS FROM ALL AROUND THE WORLD.

THE MONEY HAS ENABLED THE CLUB TO INITIATE A THRIVING JUNIOR SECTION AND, FINALLY, TO MOVE TO NEW PREMISES.'

Card fades. A final one appears.

'THE STAMFORD MODEL RAILWAY SHOW 2022 WAS THE FIRST SINCE THE ATTACK. PRIDE OF PLACE WENT TO ONE DISPLAY IN PARTICULAR:

WOODCROFT – '

Video of the layout at the show, briefly appears on the gauze, then fades.

Then, a shout across the dimming of the light.

ONE, TWO, THREE, FOUR! 'Up Yer Bum' by Peter and the Test Tube Babies plays, loud.

Blackout.

The End.